Studies in Writing & Rhetoric

Other Books in the Studies in Writing & Rhetoric Series

Language Diversity in the Classroom

Language Diversity in the Classroom

From Intention to Practice

Edited by Geneva Smitherman
and Victor Villanueva

Foreword by Suresh Canagarajah

SOUTHERN ILLINOIS UNIVERSITY PRESS

Carbondale

Copyright © 2003 by The Conference on College Composition and
Communication of the National Council of Teachers of English
All rights reserved
Printed in the United States of America
06 05 04 03 4 3 2 1

Publication partially funded by a subvention grant from The Conference on College
Composition and Communication of the National Council of Teachers of English.

Library of Congress Cataloging-in-Publication Data

Language diversity in the classroom : from intention to practice / edited by Geneva
Smitherman and Victor Villanueva ; foreword by Suresh Canagarajah.
   p. cm.
  Includes bibliographical references and index.
  1. English language—Rhetoric—Study and teaching—United States. 2. English
language—Composition and exercises—Study and teaching—United States. 3.
English language—Variation—English-speaking countries. 4. English language—
Study and teaching—Foreign speakers. 5. English language—Variation—Foreign
countries. 6. English language—Variation—United States. 7. Language and culture—United States. I. Smitherman, Geneva, date. II. Villanueva, Victor.
PE1405.U6L36 2003
808′.042′071173—dc21   2002155100
ISBN 0-8093-2532-2 (pbk. : alk. paper)

Printed on recycled paper. ♻

The paper used in this publication meets the minimum requirements of American
National Standard for Information Sciences—Permanence of Paper for Printed Library Materials, ANSI Z39.48-1992. ⊚

Contents

Foreword

Suresh Canagarajah

The articles in this monograph take stock of the progress we have made since the Conference on College Composition and Communication's 1974 resolution on "Students' Right to Their Own Language" and the 1988 resolution articulating a National Language Policy. The authors, all members of CCCC's Language Policy Committee, clearly demonstrate that the issues surrounding students' language rights are every bit as important now as they were in earlier decades. Their survey of our national organization's membership shows that language rights issues are still vexing and controversial. Their description of the scope of language issues emphasizes the ongoing presence of multiple versions of English in all our classrooms, linked to real issues of personal and ethnic identity. Their pedagogical suggestions provide hope for facilitating diversity in education and literacy. In these comments, I want to celebrate the importance of the work in this volume, especially in the context of an increasingly complicated global situation for English and language rights. While the social changes we see around us make an appreciation of CCCC's controversial pedagogical statements somewhat easier, they also recontextualize these statements, deepening their implications, creating higher levels of expectancy, and posing fresh challenges.

Consider the changes in communication and literacy. A complex of forces, including the globalization of economy and industry, transnational communities, the post-Fordist work place, and the Internet, have compelled us to shuttle across linguistic boundaries. The strict separation of locations, institutions, and roles, with distinct codes attached to each, has been breached. All of us are required to navigate different discourses in everyday domains, such as the mass media, communication, and work. The fluid social and communicative environments have motivated some educators to speak of a basic need for *multiliteracies* to be functional in today's world (Cope and Kalantzis). To be literate on the Internet, for example, requires competence in not only multiple modalities of communication (sound, speech, video, and photographs, in addition to writing) and multiple symbol systems (icons, images, color, and charts, in addition to words) but also multiple registers, discourses, and languages. In such a context, we readily recognize that teaching literacy in a single language (English) or a single dialect of that language ("standard English") fails to equip our students for real world needs. It is not surprising, therefore, that a majority of the teachers responding to the Language Knowledge and Awareness Survey, conducted by CCCC's Language Policy Committee, agree in sentiment with the need for language diversity.

However, these social changes also complicate the challenge. The "students' language" that the 1974 resolution aimed to validate was that of less privileged groups in this country. But the globalization of English has forced us to take account of many other variants from other parts of the world, represented by our students. Their grammatical systematicity, social functionality, and postcolonial ideological vibrancy have been well articulated. Moreover, they are gaining more currency than the traditionally recognized "native" dialects. There is statistical backing to the claim that native speakers "lost their majority in the 1970's" (Graddol 58). Projecting that by the year 2050, native speakers of English will be 433 million while those who have nativized the language will be 668 million, David Graddol goes on to argue in "The Decline of the Native Speaker" that "in future [English] will be a language used mainly in multilingual contexts as a second language and for communication between non-native speakers" (57). This means that we must not only make spaces for the Englishes that our Indian, Singaporean, Nigerian, and Jamaican students bring to the classroom but also increase an awareness of these codes among monolingual "native" students.

Students' right to their own language may even have to include

languages other than English—the vernaculars of many other communities represented in our classrooms. What about our students'
right to their Chinese, Korean, Japanese, and Spanish? This question receives urgency as we now see before us the effects of transnational life. Our students from Hong Kong, Korea, Japan, and the
Hispanic world shuttle frequently between the United States and
their countries of origin. These students desire equal facility in English and their national languages. We cannot teach them English
literacy without relevance to the other languages they use in their
everyday life. (To do this, we don't have to be proficient in those
languages.) The reality of hybrid texts and fluid literacies increases
the possibility that these languages will find equal yet mixed functionality in many contexts of postmodern communication. With the
boundedness and self-confinement of the nation gradually eroding
as the global seeps into the local, one might question whether we
can have an exclusive "national" policy on anything anymore without being sensitive to the pressures and pulls of the international.
Accommodating diverse languages/dialects in education is not a
compassion we show for minority students; it is becoming a matter
of economic necessity even for monolingual students from dominant social groups.

It will be sad indeed if these social developments serve only to
arm us with a fashionable discourse of multiculturalism—one that
may serve to cover up our inadequacies in educational practice. But
this is what Tove Skutnabb-Kangas discovers in her extensive review of performance by countries in implementing linguistic human rights, especially in the context of the 1953 UNESCO declara-
tion on the right of every child to be educated in the vernacular. She
observes: "Often, language is present in the lofty non-duty-inducing
phrases in the preambles of the HRs [Human Rights] instruments
but disappears completely in the educational parts of these documents" (185). Similarly, within education itself, she finds inconsistencies between intention and practice. After a careful analysis of
the stated positions and results of implementation, she concludes
with her rating of countries according to their achievement. Among

her findings is the following: "Today's unipolar big superpower, United States . . . is among the 30 worst countries, with all 'rogue states' except North Korea faring better" (200). Skutnabb-Kangas goes on to argue that Western countries, which adopt the moral high ground for championing democratic rights and liberal values around the world, do not live up to their claims when it comes to implementing linguistic rights in their own communities.

Surprisingly, many "underdeveloped" countries with countless language groups provide more facilities for vernacular education compared to those that are economically better endowed and linguistically less diverse. Papua New Guinea, the nation with probably the largest number of languages, boasting about 800 among its population of five million people, provides education in some 380 languages, plus Pidgin, to its kindergarteners and first and second graders. A researcher assesses: "Children become literate more quickly and easily in their mother tongues than they did in English. They also appear to learn English more quickly and easily" (Klaus; qtd. in Skutnabb-Kangas 179). There are other inspiring stories of individual achievement from diverse local contexts here in the United States. A Chinese American student who is tongue-tied in his English as a Second Language (ESL) class, stigmatized for his "broken English," interacts freely in many English dialects with Internet buddies from all over the world, eventually developing the motivation and aptitude to master Standard American English (Lam). A Japanese graduate student who finds the dominant modes of argumentation in her discipline too antagonistic for her tastes adopts a non-adversarial mode of argumentation that provides a critical edge to her dissertation and challenges her mentors (Belcher). A Chinese faculty member, marginalized when she uses either her "native" discourse or the dominant Anglo-American academic discourse, explores a "third space" that draws from the resources of both English and Chinese to construct a more confident and critical prose (Li). From such reports, we learn the paradoxical truth that the vernaculars are a resource and a valued addition to mainstream literacy.

That pedagogical practice has failed to be shaped by these in-spiring stories is partly because it is still guided by outworn para-digms. We cannot pour new wine into old skins. My colleagues in ESL are beginning to abandon the distinctions "native"/"nonnative" or "standard"/"non standard" and treat everyone as speakers of Global English—a multinational language featuring a plural gram-matical system with diverse norms and conventions in different communities. (Of course, there are expert and novice users of these Englishes, with different degrees of fluency and competence.) We realize that rather than judging divergence as error, we should ori-entate to it as an exploration of choices and possibilities. Rather than teaching *rules* in a normative way, we should teach *strategies*—creative ways to negotiate the norms operating in diverse contexts. Rather than developing mastery in a "target language," we should strive for competence in a repertoire of codes and discourses. Rather than simply joining a speech community, we should teach students to shuttle between communities. Not satisfied with teaching stu-dents to be context-sensitive, we should teach them to be context-transforming.

Of course, translating these orientations to the classroom takes creativity, daring, and patience. Informed by developments in wider social and pedagogical contexts, we have to focus on the local situa-tion of our own specific students and classrooms. It is from this per-spective that the stories of the educators in this monograph will be carefully read by those inside and outside composition. The authors' call for better language rights education for teachers of English at all levels, for instance, has real implications across both the nation and the globe. Many of the pedagogical suggestions described in the last half of this volume can enhance teaching in a wide range of con-texts. In fact, if postmodern globalization, the new role of English, and multiliteracies have made the challenges facing all of us similar, we can also share teaching resources with each other. Those who lack the imagination to apply the perspectives and practices nar-rated here to their own pedagogical contexts should at least go away with one important observation: that among the American teachers buried under Skutnabb-Kangas's unfavorable statistics on linguistic human rights, there are at least some who are struggling honestly to make spaces for the vernacular in their classrooms.

Works Cited

Belcher, Deborah. "An Argument for Nonadversarial Argumentation: On the Relevance of the Feminist Critique of Academic Discourse to L2 Writing Pedagogy." *Journal of Second Language Writing* 6.1 (1997): 1–21.

Cope, Bill, and Mary Kalantzis, eds. *Multiliteracies: Literacy Learning and the Design of Social Futures*. New York: Routledge, 2000.

Graddol, David. "The Decline of the Native Speaker." *AILA Review* 13 (1999): 57–68.

Klaus, D. "The Use of Indigenous Languages in Early Basic Education in Papua New Guinea: A Model for Elsewhere?" *Language and Education: An International Journal*. In press.

Lam, Eva Wan Shun. "L2 Literacy and the Design of the Self: A Case Study of a Teenager Writing on the Internet." *TESOL Quarterly* 4.3 (2000): 457–82.

Li, Xiao-Ming. "Writing from the Vantage Point of an Outsider/Insider." *Non-Native Educators in English Language Teaching*. Ed. G. Braine. Mahwah, NJ: Erlbaum, 1999. 43–56.

Skutnabb-Kangas, Tove. "Marvelous Human Rights Rhetoric and Grim Realities: Language Rights in Education." *Journal of Language, Identity, and Education* 1.3 (2002): 179–206.

Resolution from "Students' Right to Their Own Language" and the National Language Policy Statement of the CCCC

The complete text of the "Students' Right to Their Own Language" was published in *College Composition and Communication* in the fall of 1974 and can be seen at <www.ncte.org/cccc/positions/right_to language.shtml>. The following is the resolution from the 1974 meeting of the Conference on College Composition and Communication:

We affirm the students' right to their own patterns and varieties of language—the dialects of their nurture or whatever dialects in which they find their own identity and style. Language scholars long ago denied that the myth of a standard American dialect has any validity. The claim that any one dialect is unacceptable amounts to an attempt of one social group to exert its dominance over another. Such a claim leads to false advice for speakers and writers, and immoral advice for humans. A nation proud of its diverse heritage and its cultural and racial variety will preserve its heritage of dialects. We affirm strongly that teachers must have the experiences and training that will enable them to respect diversity and uphold the right of students to their own language.

An extended text of the National Language Policy, including Background Statement, can be seen at <www.ncte.org/cccc/positions/ national_language_policy.shtml>. The policy itself is as follows:

Be it resolved that CCCC members promote the National Language Policy adopted at the Executive Committee meeting on March 16, 1988. This policy has three inseparable parts:
1. To provide resources to enable native and nonnative speakers to achieve oral and literate competence in English, the language of wider communication.
2. To support programs that assert the legitimacy of native languages and dialects and ensure that proficiency in one's mother tongue will not be lost.
3. To foster the teaching of languages other than English so that native speakers of English can rediscover the language of their heritage or learn a second language.

Language Diversity in the Classroom

Introduction

Geneva Smitherman and Victor Villanueva

This monograph is about language and racism, about language and nationalism, about discussing and teaching the connections between language and racism and nationalism. Every essay in this collection asks us to think about how we enact our belief in the multiplicity of language, of English, in our classrooms.

Victor gets an e-mail question from a graduate student:

> Why do you call yourself an "American" academic of Color in the title of your book? Why not a Puerto Rican in the U.S. academy? Or an American academic? Or something a little less . . . "American?"

A response:

> This is not an unreasonable question from a Rican. And *Bootstraps* [a book by Victor] does address this in any number of ways. But I'll answer it this way. I was born in Brooklyn. Raised there with Black kids and Asian kids and one Mexican kid and Boricuas. My first language was Spanish; my first English was the English of the neighborhood, Black and Spanglish, or even a Black Spanglish. When I was 15, the family moved to California. I've been in the West (except for two years in Kansas City and trips abroad) ever since—with Mexican kids, Chicano kids, vato kids, pachuco kids,[1] Indian kids, Asian kids, Black kids, and White kids. And the nonsense that Ricans have to endure in New York is the same nonsense that all the other kids of Color endure. And I wanted that understood ("ethno-nation" is

Ramon Grosfoguel's language). Or let me do a variation of Tato Laviera:

My tongue is Boricua
My ear is Boricua and Black
My being in this country is Color
even though
My skin is white.

I'm a Puerto Rican and a portorican (the way we say it in New York) but with all those crazy mixes of the ghetto. I can never be just simply American, even though Boriquen Arawak Taino is America. For here, this place where I have lived my life, I am a person of Color. And you are too while you're here, but you have a home to go to—Puerto Rico—and in a very real sense, I do not. My parents do—Río Piedras y Caguas. But I don't. I'm a Nuyorican. But to get the point across, an Academic Nuyorican wouldn't have drawn the same number of readers, and my last 53 years have been all of it but White—Color, Latino, Nuyorican with a mythic homeland I've visited but have never really known—Puerto Rico. How's that?

victor.

It's one conversation about the languages that reside with one man. But he's not alone. In fact, those like him are in our classrooms in unprecedented numbers. And we know we want to celebrate their linguistic deftness. Yet we tend to hold to the belief that there is but one tongue that must be mastered if those students before us are to succeed, the standardized American English, the conventions of an universalized Edited American English. It doesn't sit well, but there it is, we say. Folks in this monograph have us think again, even tell us what we might do in our classrooms.

Sociologists Eduardo Bonilla-Silva and Tyrone A. Forman question the many research studies performed since 1964 that demonstrate that racial attitudes in the United States are continually getting better, or are at the least "ambivalent" and "tolerant." They point to the degree to which well-articulated, methodologically sound research questionnaires seem to demonstrate America's changing attitude away from the racism of yore. Bonilla-Silva and Forman then created their own questionnaire, distributing it to more than 400 White students at a Midwestern university. As predicted, the students demonstrated the kind of "Color-blind" ideology we would all hope for in the students (in our world, for that matter). The researchers then did in-depth interviews with a small sample, 10 percent, of those who had filled out the questionnaire. What the researchers discovered is that *appearing* racist is the taboo, not racism itself. Rather than being Color-blind, what arises is a Color-blind racism, a racism that, borrowing from Sartre, refuses to name itself (Sartre having called the bourgeoisie the class that refuses to name itself). The students interviewed "use a new *racetalk* to avoid appearing 'racist'" (Bonilla-Silva and Forman 50). The new racism is a "competitive racism." "Equality" becomes "meritocracy." That folks of Color don't achieve the same status as Whites in equal numbers (or comparable ratios) becomes part of racial pathologies, replete with a list of "if only" statements ("If only they'd stop whining and get to work"). No one wants to appear racist. Too many refuse to acknowledge that the systemic problems of racism continue. The Bonilla-Silva and Forman article's title? "'I Am Not a Racist but . . .': Mapping White College Students' Racial Ideology in the USA."

"I'm not racist, but if those kids want to get ahead, they need to learn proper English."

This monograph grew out of a concern that the Conference on College Composition and Communication's "Students' Right to Their Own Language" and the CCCC National Language Policy were no longer recognized. The history of both documents marks the opening chapter to the monograph, written by an active agent in their production, Geneva Smitherman. This sets the stage for a discussion of the Language Knowledge and Awareness Survey, conducted by the CCCC Language Policy Committee, also headed by Smitherman. As Elaine Richardson will detail in the second chapter, the overwhelming majority of those surveyed believe that the country's

dialects and languages are worthy of respect, that at least outside the
schools, dialects and languages other than the American prestige—
standardized American English and its written form, Edited American English—should be maintained and nurtured to the extent that
that is possible. As would be expected, the greatest support for
the maintenance of other-than-standard dialects and for languages
other than English comes from those surveyed who self-identified
as people of Color. Significantly, the majority of those surveyed,
while believing in the need for training in linguistic diversity, were
unaware of the published positions of their professional organizations along those lines.

Despite the general attitude reported in the survey, the attitudes
concerning the specifics of teaching make it clear that the training
of English teachers—at all levels—ought to include a course on language awareness and on American dialects. The commonly taken
course on the history of the English language apparently doesn't go
far enough. A simple knowledge of the diverse linguistic history
of English does not appear to translate sufficiently into classroom
practice with the kind of resonance suggested by those who had had
training in American dialects or African American Language. For
that matter, the very notion of a standardized English is itself worth
reviewing. In chapter 3, Victoria Cliett takes us outside the confines
of this country to discuss the nationalism implicit in a standard
English, noting that a global English means that there are World
Englishes, many standards. As English expands, so should our practices.

With chapter 4, we move into the classroom. Arnetha F. Ball and
Rashidah Jaami` Muhammad discuss racetalk in a teacher prepara-
tion class, noting the emergence of a "zero tolerance" to linguistic
diversity in the classroom in the discussion of a group of preservice
teachers. Ball and Muhammad offer a solid suggestion for teacher
preparation programs. Kim Brian Lovejoy, in chapter 5, provides
some practical suggestions for discussing linguistic diversity in first-
year college composition courses, suggestions that seem transport-
able to other grade levels.

Finally, Gail Y. Okawa offers the theoretical foundation for a language course based on the autobiographical, asking that we ask our students to consider the experiences and writing of writers of Color. All this is followed by a bibliography compiled by C. Jan Swearingen and Dave Pruett so that we might learn more about language, languages, and language diversity.

Yet this isn't a book about the teaching of English as a foreign or a second language. We will read about Singapore English and Hawaiian "Pidgin," about *la Frontera* and New York City (at least three boroughs), even about a maple syrup farm and the dialect of the U.S. Northeast—Englishes all. We will of course discuss African American Language. We who teach English language arts really should know something about African American Language after so many decades, after all. We should. Yet the analyses presented throughout and the pedagogies discussed throughout will go beyond African American Language speakers to language variation more generally. The folks in these pages have thought some about the contradictions between our intentions and our practices (and the practical considerations that give rise to our practices). They deliver strong messages on how we might bring our intentions and practices into line, to work with and within linguistic variety.

Runa Pacha
The feeling grows for weeks
before I realize
what has happened.
I got lost in the white
of concrete and motors
where I hadn't heard a hint
of unaccented Spanish in days,
just guttural clipped tones,
news of lines drawn close,
news of laws to drive
the undocumented south.
An unexpected melody
from a bamboo flute,
a quena tuned to the key

of la, falls into the crack.
My lips curl like a cat's
better to taste the sound
with my teeth. I round
my tongue to say *mucho gusto,*
igualmente, but the flaccid muscles
catch on oval tones.
Panicked, I swear to grow
my hair again, let that hank
hang down my back.
I swear to begin each day
with songs sung in softer oooo's,
rolling rrrr's, lilting llll's, rub awake
the parts I've learned to muffle
in this inhospitable air.

—Diana García

Note

The poem "Runa Pacha" is from *When Living Was a Labor Camp* by Diana García. © 2000 Diana García. Reprinted by permission of the University of Arizona Press.

1. *Pachuco* and *vato* are Chicano self-references, the pachuco being a Chicano who wore zoot suits in the 1940s and now a reference to one who dresses "Chicano-style," and the vato being the Chicano equivalent to "homey" or "dude." Neither of these terms translate into the Puerto Rican ghetto cultures of my childhood.

Works Cited

Bonilla-Silva, Eduardo, and Tyrone A. Forman. "'I Am Not a Racist but . . . ':
    Mapping White College Students' Racial Ideology in the USA." *Discourse
    and Society* 1 (2000): 50–85.
CCCC Language Policy Committee. *Language Knowledge and Awareness Sur-
    vey.* Final Report (corrected copy). Jan. 2000 <http://www.ncte.org/cccc/
    langsurvey.pdf>.

1 / The Historical Struggle for Language Rights in CCCC

Geneva Smitherman

Among the language arts crowd, the Conference on College Composition and Communication has become famous (or infamous, depending on your vantage point) for its 1974 "Students' Right to Their Own Language" resolution. However, virtually since its inception, CCCC has served as the site of dialogues about language issues. Through its journal—initially called its "official bulletin"—publications, conferences, and annual conventions, CCCC has consistently provided a forum for discussion and debate about language controversies. The recent national membership survey conducted by the Language Policy Committee is thus situated within a fifty-year history of CCCC involvement in language rights struggles. In fact, although the organization has not always stepped decisively and swiftly to the challenge, its past record as advocate for those on the linguistic margins is, on balance, one in which CCCC can take pride. This chapter will discuss the historical and intellectual background of CCCC's role in language controversies and locate the organization's major language policies—"Students' Right" and National Language Policy—within a sociopolitical context.

Donald J. Lloyd and the "New Linguistics"

We begin this journey with the words of linguist Donald J. Lloyd:[1]

> The [article] is an expression at the very least of a frivolous obscurantism, or at the most of a vigorously cultivated ignorance. . . . Failure to know [the factual studies of language] and what they mean . . . is responsible for the fact that the educational heart of darkness . . . is the English

course. . . . Emphasis on "correctness"—at the expense . . . of a fluid, knowledgeable command of our mother tongue —is responsible for the incompetence of our students in handling their language, for their embarrassment about their own rich . . . dialects, for their anxiety when they are called upon to speak or write . . . and for their feeling that the study of English is the study of trivialities which have no importance or meaning outside the English class. . . . In our day, to make statements about English and about language which do not square with linguistics is professionally reprehensible. Yet it is an indulgence arrogantly and willfully permitted themselves by many English teachers, not decently hidden in class, but in open publication in the journals of our field and in the concoction of the dreariest collection of ignorantly dogmatic textbooks that dominates any discipline in the schools. ("Darkness" 10–12)

Thus Lloyd launched the first debate in the pages of *College Composition and Communication (CCC)*. It was February 1951, and CCCC was just two years old. Lloyd was replying to "The Freshman Is King; or, Who Teaches Who?," which had been published in the December 1950 issue of *CCC* by Kenneth L. Knickerbocker of the University of Tennessee-Knoxville. In his scathing critique, with its signifyin title, "Darkness Is King," Lloyd took Knickerbocker to task for coming to conclusions about nineteen "controversial" expressions (for example, *Who did you meet?*) based on an opinion survey by a layperson published in *Harper's Magazine*. Lloyd argued that the "disputed expressions" had all been studied and "found to be in good use in this country," and he stated unequivocally that "the language of a person who uses none of these expressions is not superior to the language of one who uses some of them, or indeed, to that of one who uses all of them" (10). Not content with just knocking Knickerbocker upside the head, Lloyd also slammed the journal and the organization: "The appearance [of this article] in the bulletin of the CCCC is a little shocking," and "The assertion or implication that the language of a person who uses none of these expressions is superior on that account is a professional error which no English teacher should commit in print, and no editor should permit him to make" (10).

Surprisingly, Knickerbocker seemed not to be offended and even gave Lloyd props for his rhetorical skills:

> This is a highly literate reply to my "frivolous obscurant-ism." It indicates that somewhere along the line Mr. Lloyd has been concerned with correctness. (I should like to teach my students to write as well as he does.) It may be that my little paper did not deserve to reap such a fine whirlwind, but since it did, let it blow. (Lloyd, "Darkness" 10, footnote)

And blow it did! Although Knickerbocker was not heard from again on the subject, Martin Steinmann Jr. came into the fray, accusing Lloyd of lapses of logic that led him to "exhortations to action" (12). He and Lloyd did battle in three issues of *CCC*. Steinmann's obtuse writing style makes his critique difficult to follow, but in the main he appears to be arguing that Lloyd has invoked linguistics as a science to tell us what people *should* say based on what they *do* say. Actually, Lloyd's argument does not take this route at all. Rather, he points out Knickerbocker's fundamental error in accepting what people *think* they say for what they *do* say. Steinmann's critique thus may be summed up as a "misguided foray into irrelevant tedious-ness and willful misconstruction of Lloyd's meaning" (Sheridan).

Clearly, from the jump, then, CCCC was a forum for linguistic debates and language issues of various kinds. To a great extent, this is attributable to the parallel development of composition/rhetoric and linguistics in the 1950s and 1960s as both fields sought to re-invent themselves and stake intellectual claim to distinct identities among the established disciplines of the academy. In those early years, linguistics was breaking away from anthropology and phi-losophy and formulating new grammars reflective of how English actually works (structural, transformational), grammars to replace the misfit Latinate-based models of old. At the time, there was a good deal of excitement about the "New Grammar," and linguistics seemed to hold out great promise to resolve a host of problems in the human sciences: language teaching and learning, the mystery of the structure of human cognition—and the teaching of literacy. Thus the most frequently cited authors in *CCC* articles in this early period were linguists, for example, Fries, Lloyd, and Chomsky. The articles generally focused on the relevance, for composition studies, of the theories and research coming out of linguistics. Within this general concern, the focus was most often on the specific issue of usage and the teaching of writing to those students who used non-standard English forms and who did not (as Fries had put it back in 1940) "carry on the affairs of the English speaking people" (12–13). In this early period, those students were typically not students of Color but were rural and/or working-class Whites. Lloyd took up the cause of these White regional and social class dialects:

> You discover . . . that dialects you have grown up to de-spise are rooted in respectable antiquity and still reflect the vicissitudes of pioneer life. If you respect American tradi-tions, you find these traditions best embodied in the lan-guage of the illiterate back-country farm families, whether they still stand on their own land or congeal in uneasy clots in our industrial cities. You come therefore to de-scribe with respect. You give information; you do not de-vise new decalogues. ("English Composition" 41)

Some scholars argued that composition courses should be built around linguistics, that the English language itself, when studied from the vantage point of the new grammatical paradigms, could well serve as the content of the composition curriculum (see, for example, Carroll, Fowler). Beginning with the proposition that "an English composition course around linguistics" would "take the English language as a social instrument expressing, conditioning, and . . . conditioned by the society that uses it," Lloyd even goes so far as to say that linguistics "is a promised land for the English teacher" ("English Composition" 40, 43). Linguist and longtime

CCCC leader Harold B. Allen, though espousing the value of linguistics, nonetheless issued a note of caution, arguing that

> [i]t is my present conviction that power in the use of language, rather than mere skill, derives from sensitive awareness of the manifold resources of language, in structure as well as in vocabulary. This conviction rests on a priori grounds; but so does the belief of those who omit linguistic content and rely upon dogma. We need evidence that comes from research. ("Linguistic Research" 57)

Ralph B. Long was not only cautious but caustic in assessing the "New Linguistics" in the composition classroom. In "Grammarians Still Have Funerals," Long questions the usefulness of the "New Grammar" for composition instruction, indicts linguists for their "odd romantic primitivism" when it comes to speech and writing, and lambastes one linguist for having declared that "a person would just as soon call himself a con man or an alchemist as a grammarian." Long rebuts:

> I have called myself a grammarian for many years. . . . Until Roberts' book came along, it would not have occurred to me to compare grammarians—or even New Linguists, in spite of the extravagant claims many of them make for their work—with con men and alchemists. . . . [T]he grammar Lloyd and Warfel and Roberts give at great length—at greater length than seems desirable for Freshman English —is about as vulnerable as the school grammar these men scorn. . . . It is unlikely that the New Linguists have really achieved immortality. (211–16)

The late linguist James Sledd, however, seems to have put the lie to Long's assertion. Often referred to as "the conscience of the field" (Olson 298), Sledd was a regular on CCCC and National Council of Teachers of English (NCTE) conference programs over the decades, during which time he consistently challenged compositionists and other language arts theorists and practitioners on behalf of linguistically marginalized and economically disenfranchised voices. In 1956, in his first appearance in *CCC*, Sledd asserted that while subordinate clauses are grammatically subordinate, this should not be confused, as it often is even today, with being logically subordinate. Thus, some teachers' admonition to put the main idea in the main clause and the subordinate idea in the subordinate clause doesn't always work. While Sledd's essay doesn't deal directly with language rights issues—a theme that he would, in the coming decades, write about eloquently and powerfully—his "Coordination (Faulty) and Subordination (Upside-Down)" is still important in our historical narrative because it offered a precise and accurate linguistic description as a corrective for the misassumptions about language that many composition and language arts teachers held (and perhaps still hold?). Thus Sledd, a stalwart of the language rights struggle, here exemplifies the contributions of the New Linguists to the then-emerging field of composition studies.

Concerning standards of usage, Charles Hartung in 1957 echoed other progressive linguists in making a case for the value of linguistics in establishing usage norms for composition students. He argued that usage should be governed by "the doctrine of the linguistic norm," a standard derived from balancing "the intention of the speaker, the nature of the language itself, and the probable effect on the audience" (62). However, while throughout the 1950s and 1960s linguists and other CCCC scholars advocated the legitimacy and adequacy of all language variations, they also consistently called for teachers to toe the line in terms of teaching the social inadequacy of nonstandard English. "If a new doctor or minister says 'you was,' confidence in him is lowered. Educated people should talk like educated people, no matter who is listening or what the occasion may be" (Ives 154). In his 1952 "Preparing the Teacher of Composition and Communication—A Report," based on his visit to forty-seven different colleges and universities, where he interviewed department heads, graduate deans, full- and part-time faculty, and graduate students, Harold Allen argued strongly that writing teachers should possess linguistic knowledge and sophistication. In virtually the same breath, however, he also advocated that instructors should "help students to substitute one set of language practices for another set" (11). This is essentially a philosophy of subtractive bilingualism and is exactly the kind of contradictory position that Ernece B. Kelly would lambaste the entire CCCC organization for in her 1968 "Murder of the American Dream" speech. Even Lloyd, often considered a linguistic radical, acknowledged that instructors would find that they had to make a "change" in their students, although, in contrast to his contemporaries, he argues for an additive bilingualism:

> If we find anything that we have to change—and we do— we know that we are touching something that goes deep into [a given student's] past and spreads wide in his personal life. We will seek not to dislodge one habit in favor of another but to provide alternative choices for freer social mobility. We seek to enrich, not to correct. . . . By respecting their traditions and the people from whom they come, we teach them to respect and to hold tight to what they have as they reach for more. ("English Composition" 42)

By 1962, as evidenced in his "On Not Sitting Like a Toad," Lloyd had refined his pedagogy for using "New Grammar" concepts (for example, pattern practice drills) to teach language habits while simultaneously promoting retention of the mother tongue. In a class all by himself in those early years in the history of CCCC, Lloyd anticipated the thinking that would lead to the "Students' Right" resolution two decades later.

"Murder of the American Dream"

One major result of the social movements of the 1960s and 1970s was the creation of educational policies to redress the academic exclusion of and past injustices inflicted upon Blacks, Browns, women, and other historically marginalized groups. Programs and policies such as Upward Bound, open enrollment, Educational

Opportunity Programs, and preferential/affirmative action admissions and the development of special academic courses ("basic writing") brought a new and different brand of student to the college composition classroom. Unlike returning military veterans and other working class White students of the 1950s, this new student spoke a language that reflected not only a different class but also a different race, culture, and historical experience.

The symbolic turning point was 1968. The assassination of Dr. Martin Luther King Jr., which occurred during the annual CCCC Convention in Minneapolis, brought the organization "shockingly to an awareness of one of its major responsibilities" (Irmscher 105). In his memorial to King in the May 1968 issue of *CCC*, editor William F. Irmscher indicated that the organization now had a "new demand" placed upon it. Although he did not put it in these terms, for the first time, race/Color as a central component of linguistic difference became an in-yo-face issue that the organization could no longer ignore. It was not that race/Color was a new issue that had somehow just fallen from the sky; rather, the organization had heretofore simply proceeded as if racial differences did not exist and as if race did not need to be taken into account in the life of CCCC. In a sense, Irmscher's half-page homage to King symbolizes CCCC's loss of innocence.

Ernece Kelly's speech, "Murder of the American Dream," was delivered at the annual meeting in Minneapolis after the announcement of King's assassination and was reprinted in the May 1968 issue of *CCC*. In this brief but powerful work, Kelly reproached CCCC for the lack of Black representation in the program, rebuked the organization for the exclusion of Black intellectual and literary products in anthologies, and took it to task for the way it was dealing with Black Language. Kelly states:

> Here we meet to discuss the dialects of Black students and how we can upgrade or, if we're really successful, just plain *replace* them. . . . Why aren't there Blacks here who will talk about the emergence of an image among Blacks which does not permit them to even bother with the question of

whether or not the white man understands their dialect? . . .
Why aren't there Blacks . . . [dealing] with the richness
and values of the language of the Black ghetto? . . . Such
ideas have been dealt with and their complexities examined. Why weren't these papers presented here? (107)

Subsequently, and as a direct response to her "Murder of the
American Dream" speech, Kelly was invited to coedit an issue of
CCC, which appeared later that year, in December 1968. That issue
includes articles by four African American writers, a first for *CCC.*
Several of the articles in this special issue, by both Black and non-
Black scholars, touch on the question of language (as well as other
cultural issues). Sarah Webster Fabio, for instance, poses the question, "What is Black Language?" Indicating that this and other culturally toned questions were frequently being asked during that
time, she defines Black Language as

> direct, creative, intelligent communication between black
> [sic] people based on a shared reality, awareness, under-
> standing which generates interaction; it is a rhetoric which
> places premium on imagistic renderings and concretiza-
> tions of abstractions, poetic usages of language, idiosyncra-
> sies—those individualized stylistic nuances . . . which . . .
> hit "home" and evoke truth. (286)

James A. Banks's "Profile of the Black American" deals with a range
of cultural issues, asserts the legitimacy of Black students' language,
and downplays the need to master "standard English":

> When evaluating their compositions, the teacher must re-
> alize that these students emanate from a different culture . . .
> which possesses a language with a different structure and
> grammar, but nevertheless a valid structure and grammar.
> Thus the teacher must concentrate on the quality of ideas
> in the composition rather than on the student's use or mis-
> use of standard American English grammar. Our mission is

to teach these students how to think, to describe their environment, and to encourage their creativity. . . . Grammar is incidental; the student will later pick up standard English grammar if he sees a need for it and if we have succeeded in developing his reflective and problem solving skills. (296)

In the same issue, Leonard Greenbaum's "Prejudice and Purpose in Compensatory Programs" predicts an Orwellian nightmare for those seeking to suppress African American speech and other language varieties.

Dialect has positive aspects . . . that are not part of standardized English. . . . The desire to eliminate dialect is an egocentric solution proposed out of power and out of traditional modes of education that have always shunned the experimental in favor of the pragmatic. This was how the "system" dealt with immigrants at the turn of the century and just prior to and during World War II, and it is how, similarly, some propose it should deal with rural or inner-city dialects in the 1960's. This desire, no doubt, will win out. I can predict what lies in our future—a uniform society, most likely in uniform. . . . [W]e are hastening to our meeting with Orwell. (305)

Elisabeth McPherson's brilliant, thoughtful piece, "Hats Off— or On—to the Junior College," employs, as a point of departure, a controversy about male students wearing their hats inside a community college building. "There was more involved than a possibly out-of-date, middle-class custom. There was a racial issue, too; it was only the Negro students for whom the hats, very narrow brimmed and often very expensive, were a badge and a symbol" (317). In the course of her discussion, she touches on the matter of language as a mark of identity and culture, citing the work of linguist Benjamin Whorf, and invokes the hat metaphor to address the question of dialects:

The question of usage . . . is very much like the question of hats. Which is the more important status symbol for the student: leaving his hat on—and keeping his own identity? Taking it off and learning to be an imitation WASP? This is a decision only the student can make. . . . If changing his dialect is not the student's own idea . . . we have no right to insist on it simply because we prefer the sound of our own. If we are a college, and not just defenders of the status quo, we've more important business than worrying about dialect changes. (322)

Three years after the publication of this essay, McPherson would become a crucial member of the "Students' Right to Their Own Language" Committee. Nearly two decades later, in 1987, she accepted appointment to the Language Policy Committee, on which she continued to serve despite a lingering and debilitating illness.

Students' Right to Their Own Language
We affirm the students' right to their own patterns and varieties of language—the dialects of their nurture or whatever dialects in which they find their own identity and style. Language scholars long ago denied that the myth of a standard American dialect has any validity. The claim that any one dialect is unacceptable amounts to an attempt of one social group to exert its dominance over another. Such a claim leads to false advice for speakers and writers, and immoral advice for humans. A nation proud of its diverse heritage and its cultural and racial variety will preserve its heritage of dialects. We affirm strongly that teachers must have the experiences and training that will enable them to respect diversity and uphold the right of students to their own language. (*Students' Right*, inside front cover)

The "Students' Right" resolution followed logically on the heels of the dramatic 1968 annual meeting of CCCC and the subsequent December 1968 special issue of *CCC*, which were themselves affected by the social movements, political events, and assassinations in the world beyond academe. The resolution is grounded in the sociolinguistic branch of linguistics, a natural affinity for CCCC. When the 1970s split in linguistics occurred, dividing the Cartesian/ formal school of linguistics (associated with Noam Chomsky) from the socially constituted school (associated with Joshua Fishman), CCCC followed the latter. As an organizational position, the "Students' Right" resolution represented a critical mechanism for CCCC to address its own internal contradictions at the same time as marching, fist-raising, loud-talking protesters, spearheaded by the Black Liberation Movement, marred the social landscape of "America the beautiful."

Some language scholars had begun to question bidialectalism as a goal for the linguistically marginalized.[2] They argued that the bidialectalism philosophy was being promoted only for those on the margins. Further, since linguistic research had demonstrated the linguistic adequacy of "nonstandard" dialects, why wouldn't the "system" accept them? To reject them was tantamount to making difference into deficiency all over again. From this viewpoint, it was clear that the charge to intellectual activists was to struggle for the wider social legitimacy of all languages and dialects and to struggle, wherever one had a shot at being effective, to bring about mainstream recognition and acceptance of the culture, history, and language of those on the margins. It was this line of thinking that moved me to get involved in CCCC and the "Students' Right" struggle; it also moved many of my peers in other fields to become involved in their respective professional organizations. Most of us had been baptized in the fire of social protest and street activism. No romantic idealists, we knew the roadblocks and limitations involved in trying to effectuate change within the system. But we also knew that without "vision, the people perish." Besides, as I commented to a fellow comrade (a psychologist, who was one of the founders of the Association of Black Psychologists), what else was we gon do while we was waitin for the Revolution to come?

In this sociohistorical climate, in the fall of 1971, CCCC officers appointed a small committee to draft a policy resolution on students' dialects. I was a member of that committee and, by the time of the 1972 vote, also a member of the CCCC Executive Committee. In March 1972, we presented the CCCC Executive Committee with the "Students' Right" position statement, a fairly terse but highly controversial (some said "explosive") paragraph. The CCCC Executive Committee passed the resolution at its November 1972 meeting, promptly enlarged the committee, and charged it with developing a background document to elaborate on the meaning and implications of the "Students' Right" policy. The Executive Committee realized that this resolution would stir up controversy and that many language arts professionals, including those teaching composition, held a variety of myths and misconceptions about language and dialects. Our job was to amass the latest scholarship and research on language diversity and on language matters relevant to the teaching of composition. The document we produced would be distributed to the membership in preparation for a vote. At the annual meeting in Anaheim, California, in April 1974, the "Students' Right to Their Own Language" was passed by a wide margin and subsequently became organizational policy. That fall, the resolution and supporting background document were published as a special issue of *CCC*.

CCCC was not merely being trendy, nor politically correct, in passing the "Students' Right" resolution. Rather, the organization was responding to a developing crisis in college composition classrooms, a crisis caused by the cultural and linguistic mismatch between higher education and the nontraditional (by virtue of Color and class) students who were making their imprint upon the academic landscape for the first time in history. In its quest to level the playing field, U.S. society was making it possible for these students from the margins to enter colleges and universities. Most of these students, however bright, did not have command of the grammar and conventions of academic discourse/"standardized English." Yet they often had other communicative strengths—creative ideas, logical and persuasive reasoning powers, innovative ways of talking about the ordinary and mundane. How was this contradiction to be resolved? What professional advice could CCCC provide to frustrated composition instructors charged with teaching this new and different student clientele how to write? What could be done to help these students succeed in the composition classroom? And in the long view, how could the composition classroom, as part of the higher education of these students, prepare them for life beyond academe? The introduction to the "Students' Right" indicates that CCCC was sharply and painfully cognizant of these issues:

> Through their representatives on Boards of Education and Boards of Regents, businessmen, politicians, parents, and the students themselves insist that the values taught by the schools must reflect the prejudices held by the public. The English profession, then, faces a dilemma: until public attitudes can be changed—and it is worth remembering that the past teaching in English classes has been largely responsible for those attitudes—shall we place our emphasis on what the vocal elements of the public think it wants or on what the actual available linguistic evidence indicates we should emphasize? (1)

In the "Students' Right" resolution and in the subsequent background document, we sought to accomplish three broad goals: to heighten consciousness of language attitudes; to promote the value of linguistic diversity; and to convey facts and information about language and language variation that would enable instructors to teach their nontraditional students—and ultimately all students—more effectively. In pursuit of these goals, the introduction of the background document posed questions that composition professionals might ask themselves:

> We need to discover whether our attitudes toward "educated English" are based on some inherent superiority of the dialect itself or on the social prestige of those who use

it. We need to ask ourselves whether our rejection of students who do not adopt the dialect most familiar to us is based on any real merit in our dialect or whether we are actually rejecting the students themselves, rejecting them because of their racial, social, and cultural origins. . . . Our major emphasis has been on uniformity, in both speech and writing; would we accomplish more, both educationally and ethically, if we shifted that emphasis to precise, effective, and appropriate communication in diverse ways, whatever the dialect? (2)

To convey facts and information about the latest research on language and language diversity, the background document was structured in the form of fifteen discussion sections, each beginning with a question implicit in the resolution. All of the fifteen questions were similar in content, if not form, to areas of concern about which members of the profession were agonizing as they sought to understand what it means, in practice, to advocate, in theory, that students have a right to their own language. The questions were:

1. What do we mean by dialect?
2. Why and how do dialects differ?
3. How do we acquire our dialects?
4. Why do some dialects have more prestige than others?
5. How can concepts from modern linguistics help clarify the question of dialects?
6. Does dialect affect the ability to read?
7. Does dialect affect the ability to write?
8. Does dialect limit the ability to think?
9. What is the background for teaching one "grammar"?
10. What do we do about handbooks?
11. How can students be offered dialect options?
12. What do we do about standardized tests?
13. What are the implications of this resolution for students' work in courses other than English?

14. How does dialect affect employability?
15. What sort of knowledge about language do English teachers need?

Finally, the background document concluded with an annotated bibliography of 129 entries keyed to the answers to the fifteen questions.

Behind the Scenes

Both supporters and detractors have assumed that the "Students' Right" Committee was comprised of like-minded individuals. Although all of us were committed to addressing the language crisis facing the new wave of students in composition classrooms and to helping resolve this crisis, there was a wide range of personal styles and great diversity in political ideologies among us. On one level, one might have considered us "progressives," but we clearly had our own internal contradictions. And so in the production of the resolution and the supporting monograph, our long hours of scholarly work were accompanied virtually every step of the way by intense political and ideological struggle.

One of our early debates occurred over the use of "his." "The Student's Right to His Own Language" was the wording of the original resolution. While a couple of the women in the group put forth strong objections to the masculinist tone, one of the men thought the whole argument was silly and a waste of time because the generic "he" had been used for centuries, and everybody knew it included women too. He then began to quote several historical examples, going way back to the Bible. One of the women interrupted this filibuster-like strategy and suggested that we should call it "Student's Right to Her Own Language," since "her" was just as generic as "he." Then we tried "his or her," but someone objected to this on grounds of verbosity. We even tried using "people," but someone remarked that we were dealing with "students," not "people," whereupon a lengthy debate ensued over whether or not the labels "people" and "students" could be used interchangeably. At the time, my Womanist consciousness was just developing, and so I was not very vocal in this hours-long debate, for which I was soundly blessed out by one of the women when we took a bathroom break. She wanted to know what kind of linguist I was who was "afraid" to challenge male hegemony. The debate was finally resolved when Elisabeth McPherson, genius that my girl was, proposed that we cast the wording in the third-person plural. We had all been so locked into our linguistic prisons that we hadn't even thought of this quite simple solution to the problem. While this issue seems old hat now in the New Millennium, lest we forget, concerns about sexism in language did not always exist—even among many women.

Nor were we of identical persuasion on the issue of America's linguistic ills and the solutions to them. Hey, some members were even opposed to the use of four-letter words among us—not just the big, bad ones, but even the little ones like "damn" and "hell." (I report with pride that I was the first to introduce "cussing" into committee discourse, to the relief of one of my male comrades.) The debates that were going on in the society, in the profession, and in CCCC about how to address America's social and sociolinguistic problems went on among us, filtered through the prism of language. Why should linguistic minorities have to learn two languages and majority members of society get by on one? That's linguistic domination. Why not accept a student paper with "nonstandard" surface features of language if the message was clear and the argument well-supported? That's what the "right" to their own language means. No, giving two grades, one for content, one for grammar, is a cop-out; you are still saying there is something "wrong" with the writer. Let's make the medium the message and write this monograph in a combination of Black English, Spanglish, and standard English. And so it went. Then, as now, for some of us, the final document is seen as equivocating; it doesn't go far enough. For others, then as now, it is perceived as too permissive.

It has been said that politics is the art of compromise. And compromise we did. After the lengthy debates and verbal duels, we finally produced a document that we all felt we could live with. Credit for blending the multiple writing styles into a readable document goes to the talented editorial hand of Richard (Jix) Lloyd-Jones and the skillful diplomacy of Melvin Butler, linguist and committee chair, whose untimely death prevented him from witnessing the fruits of his labor.[3]

Reactions to "Students' Right"

The fallout was tremendous. Stringent, vociferous objections were put forth. There were calls for the resolution to be rescinded and the background document recalled. Some blasted CCCC for abdicating its responsibility and pandering to "wide-eyed" liberals in the field. Others accused CCCC of a "sinister plot" to doom speakers of "divergent" dialects to failure in higher education by telling them that their stigmatized language was acceptable. A few simply said that CCCC had done lost they cotton-pickin minds.

On the other hand, there were many who embraced the spirit of the resolution. They thanked CCCC for the supporting document, which many found extremely helpful, even as they acknowledged its flaws. Some complimented the organization for its "moral and professional courage." Others stepped to the challenge of developing writing assignments to "tap the potential" of their marginalized students. A few simply asked CCCC why it took yall so long.

Ideas about student-centered approaches to composition instruction and about sensitivity to students' language/dialects have by now become fairly commonplace in the discourse community of composition and in the language arts profession generally—which is not to say that everyone subscribes to these ideas today, just that talk about them is no longer perceived as "weird." However, in the context of the 1970s, to promulgate ideas about students' right to *anything* was a bold, new style of pedagogy. Such ideas elicited strong reactions among CCCC professionals (irrespective of whether they supported the resolution or not) and moved the intellectual production of knowledge in the field to a whole nother level. Articles and commentaries on the "Students' Right," written in the years immediately following the resolution's passage, contain some of the most creative teaching ideas and are some of the most innovatively written essays published in *CCC* to date. David W. Cole employed the story of the Gileadites versus the Ephraimites as a metaphor to argue against the resolution. In the biblical account, the Ephraimites couldn't pronounce the word "shibboleth" in the correct Gileadite accent and could thus be prevented from crossing over the Jordan River. Similarly, Cole argued that nonmainstream dialect speakers will be prevented from crossing into the mainstream. Lawrence D. Freeman examined constitutional amendments and court cases that provide legal justification for students' right to their own language. Citing such cases as *Wisconsin v. Yoder* and *Griggs v. Duke Power,* Freeman argued that language rights can be seen as protected by custom and that there is a legal basis for hiring instructors who are skilled in the dialect/language of the students they will instruct. Seeking to devise teaching assignments grounded in the legitimacy of the students' language, Lou Kelly devised a method of "copyreading," which emphasizes clarity of meaning and expressiveness rather than grammatical correctness. Students can discover for themselves places where their writing should be edited for clarity and power, thus demonstrating, according to Kelly, that a composition instructor can facilitate students' competency in standardized English while simultaneously respecting their own idiolects. Allen N. Smith argued that "no one has a right to his own language" (155), that the resolution is a contradiction in terms, for language is a social act. William G. Clark critiqued the background document for what he deemed hypocrisy in its recommendation that teachers inform students preparing for certain occupations about the necessity of Edited American English (EAE). Clark asserted that this undermines "the resolution's claim about all dialects being equally valuable, implicitly valorizes Standardized English, and is a cop-out on the part of CCCC" (217).

The organization held its ground. It did not revoke the resolution, nor did it recall the background document. (In fact, that twenty-nine-year-old document is still in print and can be ordered from NCTE.) Some folk, ever resistant to change, continued to rail against the policy. However, the initial hysteria faded, and fewer articles and commentary about the resolution appeared in *CCC* after about 1977. Instead, many in the field, fully cognizant that marginalized students were in higher education to stay—and would, in a matter of years, become the majority of the student population—began to direct their energies to creative and pedagogically responsible ways of implementing a "Students' Right" philosophy in their composition and language arts classes. As Donald Stewart would put it a few years later, the challenge is "how to respect the dialect the student brings to school yet not avoid the responsibility of teaching him or her alternative dialects and editing skills for coping with different language situations" (330).

The "Students' Right to Their Own Language" was a policy formulated to address the contradictions developed in the midst of a major paradigm shift in higher education, itself the result of a major paradigm shift in the social order. Language arts professionals across the nation and on all levels were encountering the new brand of students and experiencing classroom crises similar to those of composition instructors. This organizational language policy opened up a national dialogue about language diversity and professional responsibility. As Richard Lloyd-Jones, longtime CCCC leader and member of both the "Students' Right" Committee and the Language Policy Committee, stated:

> The statement had an intellectual base in sociolinguistics, but its energy came from support of social diversity. It forced a reconsideration of "correctness." It implied a model of language as "transactional" rather than as artifact. Behind the anger of the political oratory was acceptance of a thesis about the nature of language. (490)

In due course, other language arts organizations adopted policies reflecting the research and scholarship on language diversity coming out of sociolinguistics. But lest we forget, CCCC was the pioneer.

CCCC During the "Second Reconstruction"

Although many compositionists and other language arts professionals greeted the "Students' Right" policy with high enthusiasm, still a great degree of lingering confusion existed: "Well, then, if I don't correct the grammatical errors, what do I do?" one well-meaning instructor queried. It seemed that the "Students' Right" background document was welcomed because it was informative in terms of theory; however, it did not go far enough in praxis. CCCC leadership acknowledged the need for something more in the form of explicit teaching materials, sample lesson plans, and a more practically oriented pedagogy. In 1976, the Executive Committee thus appointed the Selection and Editorial Committee for Activities Supporting "Students' Right to Their Own Language," on which three of the original "Students' Right" Committee members—Elisabeth McPherson, Jix Lloyd-Jones, and I—served. This new committee was charged with assembling, for publication, practical classroom assignments, activities, lectures, and teaching units that would show and tell how to apply the philosophy of the "Students' Right" resolution to the day-to-day experience of teaching and learning. By 1980, our committee had more than enough material for what we felt would be a valuable sequel to the "Students' Right" document. However, despite having spent nearly four years compiling and editing some excellent material, solicited from practitioners at all levels of language arts education, we were informed that CCCC had "reluctantly decided" not to publish the collection. What had happened since the passage of the original "Students' Right" resolution by CCCC Executive Committee (in 1972) and CCCC membership (in 1974) is attributable in great measure to the changed national climate of the 1980s.

Owing to the sociopolitical, educational, and economic decline in Black and other historically disenfranchised communities during the 1980s, political theorists such as Ronald W. Walters have dubbed the years from 1980 to 1992 the "Second Reconstruction." The "first" Reconstruction had been launched in the late 1870s, with the federal government's abandonment of ex-slaves to Southern governments, which promptly rolled back the freedmen's political gains and ushered in an era of lynchings and brutal assaults against Blacks that would not be redressed until the Black Freedom Struggle of the 1960s. After the promise and some fulfillment of the social movements of the 1960s and 1970s, the United States moved to a more conservative climate on the social, political, and educational fronts—a move solidified in 1980 by the election of Ronald Reagan. By that time, the mood of CCCC, like the mood of America, seemed to have shifted from change and promise to stagnation and dreams deferred.

It was within the climate of the Second Reconstruction that Thomas J. Farrell's 1983 bombshell, "IQ and Standard English," appeared in *CCC*. Farrell re-raised the old linguistic-cognitive deficiency theory about speakers of what was then still being called "Black English." (Although the term "Ebonics" was coined in 1973, it didn't catch on until the Oakland School Board's December 1996 resolution.) Even though Farrell asserted that "mean IQ difference" between "black ghetto children" and speakers of "standard English" has "nothing to do with genetics or race, per se" (481), still he contended that

> [t]he non-standard forms of the verb "to be" in . . . Black English may affect the thinking of the users. . . . Black ghetto children do not use the standard forms of the verb "to be." . . . Many of those same black ghetto children have difficulty learning to read, and they do not score highly on measures of abstract thinking. . . . I am hypothesizing that learning the full standard deployment of the verb "to be" is integral to developing Level II thinking because the deployment of that verb played a part in the development of abstract thinking in ancient Greece. (477, 479)

As shocking as it was to see Farrell's article in *CCC*, it has played a crucial role in the language rights debate for two reasons. First, it is a reminder that old arguments, assumed to be dead and long since buried, can resurface in new and potentially more dangerous forms that distort current research for "supporting" evidence. Second, despite my Lloydian reaction to this article's appearance in *CCC,* and notwithstanding my disillusionment about CCCC's rejection of the 1980 "Students' Right" follow-up publication, it is significant to note that by 1983 there had emerged a critical mass of compositionists who could and did provide solid, valuable rebuttals to Farrell, relying on research from sociolinguistics. And further, it is significant that *CCC* allowed the publication of four very lengthy "Counterstatement" essays in its December 1984 issue. One was from Karen Greenberg, who argued in her brilliant response that "be" verb constructions are simply applied according to different but identifiable rules of African American Language and that Farrell's terminology, such as "paratactic" and "hypotactic," was "pseudo-scientific," adding only the "gloss of respectability" (458).

National Language Policy

In the 1998 celebration of African American History Month, a television commercial for Mickey D's (Ebonics for McDonald's) featured a White father and his young son browsing through a gallery with paintings of African American heroes and she-roes. The father pointed to the work of Jacob Lawrence and told his kid, "That's Jacob Lawrence, a famous painter." Next, they come upon a painting of Harriet Tubman, and the father says, "That's Harriet Tubman, a leader in the Underground Railroad." The kid exclaims, "Wow, that's cool," as a voice-over says, "It's not just Black history, it's *American* history" (emphasis Mickey D's).

Much like the theme of the McDonald's commercial, and the legacy of Dr. Martin Luther King Jr., CCCC's National Language Policy is a linguistic imperative for all groups—not just Blacks, Browns, the poor, and others on the margins. While addressed to and for all citizens, the National Language Policy is not a repudiation of the "Students' Right" resolution. That policy was the right move for that historical period, and it filled a deep pedagogical void. The National Language Policy symbolizes the evolution of CCCC sociolinguistic consciousness and was the next logical stage after the "Students' Right" campaign.

In the fall of 1986, California passed its English Language Amendment to the state constitution, making it the first state in contemporary times to establish, by law, a policy of "English Only." S. I.

Hayakawa, at the time a member of the U.S. Senate, had introduced the first constitutional amendment on this issue in 1981, but it had stagnated in congressional committees. The proponents of English Only had thus decided to take their campaign to various states with the goal of securing the requisite number of state language amendments to give English Only the status of an amendment to the U.S. Constitution. California, with its large number of Spanish speakers and Asian and Mexican immigrants, had been selected as the test case.

A number of organizations and caucuses opposed California's measure and the growing formation of an English Only movement. Within CCCC, the opposition came during the 1987 convention from the Progressive Composition Caucus (PCC). The caucus described itself as a group of

> composition instructors who view writing as a potentially liberating activity and teach from a socialist-feminist perspective. Our curriculum often emphasizes non-canonical literature and exposes sexist, racist, homophobic and corporate manipulation of language. (*PCC Newsletter*)

Although PCC wanted CCCC to take a stand against English Only, there was also sharp tension at the time between PCC and the CCCC Executive Committee and leadership over the issue of conducting the convention in a hotel involved in a labor action. Uncertain if they could trust CCCC to do the right thing, PCC decided that their sense-of-the-house motion not only should call for concerted opposition against English Only but also should include the name of someone they trusted to carry out the mandated opposition. The day before the annual meeting, PCC asked me if I would accept the charge and if I would allow my name to be included in their resolution. As I listened to their arguments, all I could think about was the dissin and doggin I had endured during the "Students' Right" years, and I kept saying "no way."

At the annual meeting in 1987, PCC submitted the following sense-of-the-house motion:

> *Preamble:* As the leading professional organization dealing with language and literacy, the CCCC should be in the forefront of the effort to decide issues of language policy. *Resolved:* That the CCCC support the NCTE resolution opposing English-only legislation by appointing a well funded task force, chaired by Geneva Smitherman, to articulate the issues and formulate and implement strategies to educate the public, educational policy-makers, and legislatures; further, that this issue receive major emphasis in the 1988 Conference theme, "Language, Self, and Society." (CCCC Minutes, 21 March 1987, 5)

The motion passed. The task force that was appointed was called the Language Policy Committee (LPC).[4] Its charge was to develop a proactive response to the English Only movement for consideration by the CCCC Executive Committee, to compile information on English Only, and to network with other professional organizations and groups mounting English Only opposition campaigns. CCCC kept its part of the bargain. The organization provided funding, full support, and resources for the LPC to carry out its charge. Our committee met over the summer of 1987 and developed the National Language Policy and a strategic implementation plan. We presented our work to the CCCC Executive Committee meeting and at the annual business meeting in March 1988, and the following resolution passed unanimously:

Background

The National Language Policy is a response to efforts to make English the "official" language of the United States. This policy recognizes the historical reality that, even though English has become the language of wider communication, we are a multilingual society. *All* people in a

democratic society have the right to education, to employment, to social services, and to equal protection under the
law. No one should be denied these or any civil rights because of linguistic differences. This policy would enable
everyone to participate in the life of this multicultural nation by ensuring continued respect both for English, our
common language, and for the many other languages that
contribute to our rich cultural heritage.

CCCC National Language Policy
Be it resolved that CCCC members promote the National
Language Policy adopted at the Executive Committee meeting on March 16, 1988. This policy has three inseparable
parts:
1. To provide resources to enable native and nonnative
   speakers to achieve oral and literate competence in English, the language of wider communication.
2. To support programs that assert the legitimacy of native
   languages and dialects to ensure that proficiency in
   one's mother tongue will not be lost.
3. To foster the teaching of languages other than English
   so that native speakers of English can rediscover the
   language of their heritage or learn a second language.
   (CCCC, *National Language Policy*)

The National Language Policy stresses the need not just for
marginalized Americans but for all Americans to be bi/multilingual
in order to be prepared for citizenship in a global, multicultural society. More than a policy for students of one particular Color or
class, the National Language Policy recognizes that the ability to
speak many tongues is a necessity for everybody.

This time, the motion of history was on our side. Negative reaction to the National Language Policy has been minimal. Further,
this organizational policy has not had to undergo the agonizing argumentation, contestation, debate—and denial—that the "Students'
Right" resolution endured. By no stretch am I saying that composi-

tionists have all been doing the right thing since the passage of the National Language Policy. What we are witnessing, though, is a developing sociolinguistic sophistication and political maturity about language rights issues. As the field of composition/rhetoric has evolved, so too has the language consciousness of CCCC professionals. Further, theorists now recognize the need to address realities relative to students' native language/dialect in the comp context, a posture that has, unfortunately, not always been the case.

Contributions from CCCC members in the period since 1988 clearly reflect a long overdue recognition of the linguistic-cultural complexity of the composition classroom and of the writing instructor's task in that classroom. Terry Dean wrote of the pedagogical difficulties facing a "monocultural teacher" in a multicultural/multilingual composition classroom and proposed strategies for creative instruction in such a classroom. Drawing on her own multivocal competence across several linguistic and cultural traditions, CCCC leader Jacqueline Jones Royster challenged us to "construct paradigms that permit us to engage in better practices in cross-boundary discourse, whether we are teaching, researching, writing, or talking with Others, whoever those Others happen to be" (37–38). Analyzing the language and literacy practices of White students, Margaret J. Marshall makes a compelling argument for a broadened notion of "diversity" and contends that "we need a way of thinking about difference in student writing as more than a simple match between a set of predetermined divisions and uses of language" (232). In sum, then, the spirit of this organizational language policy is a broad-based challenge to address linguistic diversity throughout the body politic, not just among those who have historically been on the margins.

If it is true, as CCCC leader Anne Ruggles Gere has asserted, that changing language attitudes is tantamount to changing a worldview, then there may not be a lot that a policy from a professional organization can do about the myths and misconceptions about language that continue to plague the struggle for language rights. One cannot erase long-held attitudes and deeply entrenched biases and stereotypes with the stroke of a pen—you know, go henceforth and sin linguistically no more. On the other hand, those who (whether consciously or unconsciously) display the negative effects of linguicism are products of the school (and the college, though in fewer numbers) because everybody goes through school. The classroom, then, is a major player in shaping language attitudes, and those classrooms that are particularly crucial for the formation of ideas about language are those on the K–12 level. And here is where CCCC, as a postsecondary organization, has, unfortunately, had very limited influence.

In 1971, after the formation of what was to become the "Students' Right" Committee, CCCC leadership and members began working within NCTE to promote the concept of the students' right to their own language. For three subsequent years, there was a concerted effort by CCCC to persuade NCTE to endorse CCCC language policy. However, this did not come to pass. Instead, at the 1974 NCTE Convention, NCTE membership passed a weak version of a language rights resolution, which distinguished spoken from written language. NCTE Resolution 74.2 "accept[s] the linguistic premise that all these dialects are equally efficient as systems of communication." However, it goes on to "affirm" that students need to learn the "conventions of what has been called written edited American English." This was a posture that CCCC deliberately and consciously sought to avoid in its policy resolution because usage, spelling, punctuation, and other "conventions" of "written edited American English" were typically the only aspects of the writing process that teachers focused on. Thus, the "Students' Right" background document had asserted that

> [d]ialect . . . plays little if any part in determining whether a child will ultimately acquire the ability to write EAE. . . . Since the issue is not the capacity of the dialect itself, the teacher can concentrate on building up the students' confidence in their ability to write. . . . If we can convince our students that spelling, punctuation, and usage are less

important than content, we have removed a major obstacle
in their developing the ability to write. (8)

Many people in the language arts field (and, I would wager,
most of those outside the field) erroneously credit NCTE with the
"Students' Right" resolution. In a review published in the very pages
of *CCC* in May 1997, Gary A. Olson stated: "While the essays in
this collection touch on a number of issues, the two pervasive concerns are bidialectalism, especially in relation to NCTE's 'Students'
Right to Their Own Language'" (298). In the *Journal of English Linguistics* special issue on Ebonics, linguist Walt Wolfram bemoaned
the persistence of negative language attitudes despite the efforts of
professional organizations:

> Furthermore, the adoption of strong position statements
> on dialect diversity by professional organizations such as
> the National Council of Teachers of English (namely, the
> statement on Students' Right to Their Own Language) . . .
> barely made a dent on entrenched attitudes and practices
> with respect to language differences. (109)

Let the record be clear: despite the Faulknerian agony and sweat of
the human spirit of many CCCC language warriors, the bitter irony
is that NCTE never passed the CCCC "Students' Right to Their
Own Language" resolution.

CCCC has had a significant historical impact as a language pioneer, initiating, way back in 1951, a national conversation on issues
of dialect and language diversity. It is crucial to have organizational
policies as weapons that language rights warriors can wield against
the opponents of linguistic democratization. Since intellectuals provide the ideological rationale for public policy, it was and is important for an organization like CCCC to go on record as supporting language rights, for these policies can and do have influence
and impact. Case in point: There was a time, up until around the
mid-1970s, that speech tests were required to qualify for entry into

university teacher education programs. People like me flunked these linguistically, culturally, and gender-biased tests and got forced into speech therapy. These tests have now been eradicated. This is a direct result of the intellectual and activist wings of the social movements of the 1960s and 1970s, manifested in the academy in research that came out of sociolinguistics and in professional organizational positions like the CCCC "Students' Right to Their Own Language." The documented spirit of resistance in the "Students' Right" and National Language Policy is an important symbol that change is possible—even within the system.

Nonetheless, CCCC cannot rest on its past accomplishments. The results of the recent national membership survey (see Richardson in this volume) indicating that only slightly more than one-third of NCTE and CCCC members were familiar with CCCC's organizational language policies mean there is work to be done, right at home. As the 1990s Oakland Ebonics controversy demonstrated, and as the mounting campaigns against bilingual education show, attacks on linguistic "minorities" are continuing right on into the New Millennium. There is a need for CCCC's continued assertion of leadership in the cause for language rights, because the struggle does indeed continue.

Notes

I would like to express my gratitude and special thanks to Dr. David Sheridan (Ph.D., English, Michigan State University), for his most capable assistance and archival work. A shout out also to David Kirkland, my student research assistant for six years and now a Ph.D. candidate in education at Michigan State University, for his efforts to make me computer literate. Any shortcomings are entirely my own doing.

1. Donald J. Lloyd, who taught for years at Detroit's Wayne State University, was a major figure in the early years of composition studies and linguistics. His Ph.D. in literature from Yale University hardly equipped him to teach literacy and language, and he notes that he learned, through trial and error over the years with his students, how to teach writing. He is coauthor of *American English in Its Cultural Setting* (1962) and is credited with coining the phrase "national mania for correctness." On a personal note, while doing the research for this article, I remembered that Lloyd had taught me introductory linguistics

at Wayne State. At the time, his ideas about language were profoundly shocking to most of his students—including me, who at the time was an untutored, fresh-from-the-ghetto, very young teenager. Being the first of my family to go beyond the seventh grade—much less college—and the one on whom the family hopes for educational success were riding, I recall being highly attracted to—but at the same time fearful of—Lloyd's "heretical" challenge to mainstream language standards.

2. See Sledd's 1969 "Bi-Dialectalism."

3. The other "Students' Right" Committee members were Adam Casmier, Ninfa Flores, Jenefer Giannasi, Myrna Harrison, Richard Lloyd-Jones (who synthesized and edited our individually written sections), Richard A. Long, Elizabeth Martin, the late Elisabeth McPherson, and Ross Winterowd. The late Robert F. Hogan and Nancy S. Prichard served as NCTE *ex officio* members.

4. The other LPC members were Elizabeth McTiernan Auleta, Ana Celia Zentella, Thomas Kochman, Jeffery Youdelman, Guadalupe Valdes, and Elisabeth McPherson. Of the original group, Ana Celia Zentella and I are still on the (now reconstituted) Language Policy Committee. Other current members are Victoria Cliett, Kim Brian Lovejoy, Rashidah Muhammad, Gail Okawa, Elaine Richardson, Jan Swearingen, Denise Troutman, Victor Villanueva, and Tracy Wensing.

Works Cited

Allen, Harold B. "Linguistic Research Needed in Composition and Communication." *CCC* 5 (1954): 55–60.

———. "Preparing the Teacher of Composition and Communication—A Report." *CCC* 3 (1952): 3–13.

Banks, James A. "A Profile of the Black American: Implications for Teaching." *CCC* 19 (1968): 288–96.

Carroll, John B. "Psycholinguistics and the Teaching of English Composition." *CCC* 7 (1956): 188–93.

CCCC Language Policy Committee. *The National Language Policy*. Urbana, IL: NCTE, 1991 (brochure).

Clark, William G. "In Responses to 'Students' Right to Their Own Language.'" *CCC* 27 (1975): 217.

Cole, David W. "An Ephraimite Perspective on Bidialectalism." *CCC* 23 (1972): 371–72.

Dean, Terry. "Multicultural Classrooms, Monocultural Teachers." *CCC* 40 (1989): 23–37.

Fabio, Sarah Webster. "What Is Black?" *CCC* 19 (1968): 286–87.

Farrell, Thomas J. "IQ and Standard English." *CCC* 34 (1983): 470–84.

Fowler, Mary Elizabeth. "Using Semantic Concepts in the Teaching of Composition." *CCC* 7 (1956): 193–97.

Freeman, Lawrence D. "*Students' Right to Their Own Language*: Its Legal Basis." *CCC* 26 (1975): 25–29.

Fries, Charles Carpenter. *American English Grammar*. New York: Appleton, 1940.

Gere, Anne Ruggles, and Eugene Smith. *Attitudes, Language, and Change*. Urbana, IL: NCTE, 1979.

Greenbaum, Leonard. "Prejudice and Purpose in Compensatory Programs." *CCC* 19 (1968): 305–11.

Greenberg, Karen. "Responses to Thomas J. Farrell 'IQ and Standard English.'" *CCC* 35 (1984): 455–60.

Hartung, Charles V. "Doctrines of English Usage." *CCC* 8 (1957): 55–63.

Irmscher, William F. "In Memoriam: Rev. Dr. Martin Luther King, Jr. 1929–1968." *CCC* 19 (1968): 105.

Ives, Sumner. "Grammatical Assumptions." *CCC* 5 (1954): 149–55.

Kelly, Ernece B. "Murder of the American Dream." *CCC* 19 (1968): 106–8.

Kelly, Lou. "Is Competent Copyreading a Violation of the 'Students' Right to Their Own Language'?" *CCC* 25 (1974): 254–58.

Knickerbocker, Kenneth L. "The Freshman Is King: Or, Who Teaches Who?" *CCC* 1 (1950): 11–15.

Lloyd, Donald J. *American English in Its Cultural Setting*. New York: Knopf, 1962.

———. "Darkness Is King: A Reply to Professor Knickerbocker." *CCC* 2 (1951): 10–12.

———. "An English Composition Course Built Around Linguistics." *CCC* 4 (1953): 40–43.

———. "On Not Sitting Like a Toad." *CCC* 13 (1962): 9–13.

Lloyd-Jones, Richard. "Who We Were, Who We Should Become." *CCC* 43 (1992): 486–96.

Long, Ralph B. "Grammarians Still Have Funerals." *CCC* 9 (1958): 211–16.

Marshall, Margaret J. "Marking the Unmarked: Reading Student Diversity and Preparing Teachers." *CCC* 48 (1997): 231–48.

McPherson, Elisabeth. "Hats Off—or On—to the Junior College." *CCC* 19 (1968): 316–22.

NCTE. Resolution 74.2. Nov. 1974. NCTE Archives, Urbana, IL <http://www.ncte.org/html>.

Olson, Gary A. "Critical Pedagogy and Composition Scholarship." *CCC* 48 (1997): 297–303.

PCC Newsletter. April 1987.

Royster, Jacqueline Jones. "When the First Voice You Hear Is Not Your Own." *CCC* 47 (1996): 29–40.

Sheridan, David. Unpublished essay, 1998.

Sledd, James. "Bi-Dialectalism: The Linguistics of White Supremacy." *English Journal* 58 (1969): 1307–15.

———. "Coordination (Faulty) and Subordination (Upside-Down)." *CCC* 7 (1956): 181–87.

Smith, Allen N. "No One Has a Right to His Own Language." *CCC* 27 (1976): 155–59.

Steinmann, Martin, Jr. "Darkness Is Still King: A Reply to Professor Lloyd." *CCC* 2 (1951): 9–12.

Stewart, Donald. "Acting on the CCCC Language Resolution and Related Matters." *CCC* 31 (1980): 330–32.

Students' Right to Their Own Language. Spec. issue of *CCC* 25 (1974): 1–32.

Walters, Ronald W. *Pan Africanism in the African Diaspora.* Detroit: Wayne State UP, 1993.

Wolfram, Walt. "Language Ideology and Dialect: Understanding the Oakland Ebonics Controversy." *Journal of English Linguistics* 26 (1998): 108–21.

2 / Race, Class(es), Gender, and Age
The Making of Knowledge about Language Diversity
Elaine Richardson

As a student of language, I am ever amazed at the rhetorical strategies of government authorities. I became particularly interested in the U.S. presidential election of 2000, the Florida ballots, and the apparent silence of Supreme Court Justice Clarence Thomas. According to a *New York Times* article by Neil A. Lewis, one of the reasons he gave to high school students for not speaking much during the oral arguments of the Supreme Court hearings on the presidential vote was that when he was a youth, people used to make fun of the Gullah that he spoke. He explained that this caused him to develop the habit of listening. It could be said, then, that Justice Thomas has been silenced, even though his vote spoke volumes. When he did finally "speak" on the matter of the election, he voted against a Florida recount that could have swayed the election in favor of then vice president Al Gore. He told high school students that politics did not enter into his vote, saying, "I plead with you that whatever you do, don't try to apply the rules of the political world to this institution [the Supreme Court]" (Lewis).

But of course, Thomas's vote and his silence were political. Both can be seen as attempts to achieve a racelessness, to appear to be apolitical, to transform the ways that his audience thought about him as a Black male who is conservative and a Republican. Histories of Black struggle for inclusion influence our reading of Thomas's silence and voting/actions. To read Thomas without noticing his silence and voting patterns is to misread the way he summons these for political purposes.

Like most Black people who grew up during the era of legal racial segregation, Thomas's "race" and Gullah language were devalued and stigmatized in nearly all mainstream environments, especially school. Researchers continue to identify various ways that African American students cope with their general devaluation in school, among them impression management (Gilyard), disidentification with achievement (Steele), oppositional resistance behaviors (Ogbu, Fine), acting White (Fordham), and attempting racelessness (Fordham). Among the survival and rhetorical strategies that Thomas adopted to overcome racial and linguistic devaluation were raceless- ness and silence. An uncritical reading of Thomas's actions would interpret his strategies as successful, since they led him to achieve a position in a powerful mainstream institution. However, upon closer examination, Thomas's situatedness can be read as self-defeat- ing or powerless. From a historical perspective, Black people and their allies fought to change oppressive public policies. Thomas is the product of a consciousness that has Black people working their way into the system, adopting or adapting dominant cultural values, gaining education and training that elevates them to positions in- side of government where they can affect change, and carrying out policies to benefit Black people as a group. Yet Thomas's silence does not allow him to fulfill this role. He appears to many to have forgotten the lessons of struggle and history, suppressing his non- institutionally sanctioned Gullah (and the values of cultural equal- ity that it represents) for institutionally sanctioned silence and the voting behavior of an arch-conservative.

As a member of several discourse communities—the Black American, the scholarly, and the language educator, among them—I found Justice Thomas's remarks on language and politics especially significant because his personal attitudes toward language, his un- derstanding of the relationship of ideology to language and public policy, his (in)actions, and the source of his attitudes affect us all insofar as he holds a powerful position in our country's highest court. The general societal devaluation of Black people's language and culture helped to shape Thomas's language attitudes. As lan- guage educators and scholars in this increasingly complex society, we must stay abreast of the source of our own language attitudes, as they may help us to revise our pedagogical approaches and influence the language attitudes and policies of future justices of the Supreme Court.

Language Knowledge and Awareness Survey

This essay summarizes and speculates about the findings of the Language Knowledge and Awareness Survey, commissioned by the Conference on College Composition and Communication and the National Council of Teachers of English to assess the language attitudes and concerns of the profession. Leading organizations in language arts passed two language policies, "Students' Right to Their Own Language" (CCCC, 1974) and the "National Language Policy" (CCCC, 1988, NCTE, 1998). These organizational language policies were designed to set the tone for policy and pedagogy development to support linguistic diversity in the classroom.

Despite such policies, experienced professionals in both organizations have expressed concern about the teaching practices and lack of academic preparation in sociolinguistic issues of today's college composition and secondary English teachers. Accordingly, the Language Policy Committee of CCCC conducted a study from 1996 to 1998 to survey the state of knowledge, training, and attitudes about linguistic diversity of the membership of the leading organizations of language arts professionals.

Related Work

The work most closely related to the survey reported here has been on language attitudes among the general public and on teachers' perceptions of students' linguistic abilities. Research suggests that one's attitude toward a language or language variety affects one's attitude toward entire groups of people associated with that language or language variety.

Teachers generally possess a greater range of language attitudes than the general public. Sledd, for instance, identified teacher attitudes ranging from denial of all standards to reverence for past linguistic traditions (qtd. in Gere and Smith). In a study of teachers in a national sample, Taylor concluded that the majority had either positive or neutral attitudes toward what he termed "Black Language."

In numerous studies, Williams and his associates found that teachers not only evaluated students on the basis of language cues but also consistently judged students along a two-dimensional model: confidence-eagerness and ethnicity-nonstandardness. By comparison with White children, Black American and Latino and Latina children were ranked low in both dimensions, and the teachers' academic expectations correlated with the rankings of the children's speech.[1] More recently, Bowie posed the question of current teacher attitudes toward "Black English." She surveyed seventy-five preservice teachers at a large urban university, 86 percent of whom were White. A majority of the responses to survey questions concerning attitudes about Black English were negative, although only 63 percent reported even minimal exposure to the subject, that exposure typically having been in a single class discussion about research on Black Language. Bowie proposed new strategies for sociolinguistic change, such as requiring preservice teachers to spend time in racially diverse schools.

Byrnes and Kiger sought to validate their Language Attitudes of Teachers Scale (LATS) by surveying teachers enrolled in university courses in Arizona, Utah, and Virginia. The researchers addressed two critical questions, only indirectly related to language: whether teachers would be willing to have a Limited English Proficient (LEP) child in their classroom, and whether teachers think LEP children are detrimental to the learning of other students. Teachers who had negative attitudes about the language abilities of the LEP children thought the presence of these children in the classroom would negatively influence the learning of other students. Based on this work and an early study, the researchers concluded that teachers' negative language attitudes are a barrier to positive learning experiences of LEP children.

Issues in the CCCC Language Policy Committee Study

The CCCC, with assistance from the NCTE Research Foundation, commissioned a study that sought to answer six broad research questions relative to matters of language diversity:

1. What academic training in language diversity have NCTE and CCCC members had? And what percentage of the membership has had such training?
2. What percentage of NCTE and CCCC members believes that academic training in language diversity is needed? What kind and to what degree?
3. What are the attitudes of NCTE and CCCC members toward language variation and bi/multilingualism?
4. What are the attitudes of CCCC and NCTE members toward their own language? What are the sources of these attitudes?
5. To what extent do members' teaching practices reflect language diversity? What kinds of practices reflect awareness of language diversity?
6. To what extent do NCTE and CCCC members support organizational positions on language diversity (for example, the "Students' Right" resolution and the "National Language Policy")?

The Questionnaire

In the fall of 1996, based on input from other English professionals in literature, language, and composition, the LPC developed a questionnaire. In the spring of 1997, we conducted a pilot study to pretest the questionnaire and ascertain its reliability. The pilot involved approximately two hundred randomly selected English professionals at college, community college, and secondary school levels and English Education majors in teacher preparation programs. All three aspects of the English curriculum—language, literature, and composition—were reflected in the areas of concentration of the pilot subjects.

In the subsequent study, after establishing the reliability and validity of the questionnaire, a random, stratified probability sample was drawn from the membership lists of CCCC and the Secondary Section of NCTE, provided by NCTE headquarters, with the total sample reflecting the larger membership of NCTE. For the Secondary Section membership list, only those members teaching in grades 9–12 were included in the sample universe. Both random samples reflect stratification along the variables available in the membership profile: ethnicity, gender, region, and number of years teaching. The sample total was 2,970; approximately 67 percent of that was from the NCTE Secondary Section and 33 percent from CCCC. (However, slightly more CCCC members returned their questionnaires than did NCTE members.) The total number of completed, returned surveys was 983. These respondents comprised the sample population for the study.

Findings of the Survey

Some of the study's most interesting findings are in the demographic categorization of responses to questions about the language attitudes of educators toward language and dialect diversity. One of the study's key bases for ascertaining attitudes about language variation and bi/multilingualism were responses to statements 1–7 of the survey, which were derived from the pilot study.

To summarize:

Statement 1: A student whose primary language is not English should be taught solely in English.
33.2% agreed; 66.8% disagreed

Statement 2: Students need to master standard English for upward mobility.
96.1% agreed; 3.9% disagreed

Statement 3: In the home, students should be exposed to standard English only.
13.2% agreed; 86.8% disagreed

Statement 4: Students who use nonstandard dialects should be taught in standard English.
89.5% agreed; 10.5% disagreed

Statement 5: There are valid reasons for using nonstandard dialects.
80.1% agreed; 19.9% disagreed

Statement 6: There are valid reasons for using languages other than English.
92.6% agreed; 7.4% disagreed

Statement 7: Students should learn grammar rules to improve their ability to understand and communicate concepts and information.
78.4% agreed; 21.6% disagreed

Attitudes Toward Language Diversity

Statement 1, "A student whose primary language is not English should be taught solely in English," resulted in 33.2 percent agreeing with the teaching of nonprimary English speakers solely in English; this group tended to be White high school teachers. Conversely, from a statistically significant standpoint, those language arts educators who tended to disagree more with the teaching of nonprimary English speakers solely in English tended to be college professors of Color. (See tables 2.1 and 2.2; here and throughout, the Pearson chi-square statistical procedure was used to measure significance, with a value of .05 or lower required for statistical significance.) Table 2.1 shows the data with regard to significant correlations.

The literature in sociolinguistics has long established the interconnectedness of ethnic or racial identities to primary languages and cultures in spite of these being in flux. Nevertheless, people

Table 2.1. Significant Demographic Categories by Agreement and Disagreement with Statement 1: "A student whose primary . . ."

Tend to Agree	Tend to Disagree	Sig.
White	People of Color (POC)	.002
Bachelor's	Doctorate	.000
NCTE	CCCC	.001
High school teacher (HS)	University teacher (Univ.)	.000

Note: Statistically significant at .05 or lower.

Table 2.2. Demographic Groups' Attitudes Toward Language Variation, Grammar, and Bi- or Multilingualism

Statement	Tend to Agree	Tend to Disagree	Sig.
1. A student whose primary language is not English should be taught solely in English.	White	POC	.002
	Bachelor's	Doctorate	.000
	NCTE	CCCC	.001
	HS	Univ.	.000
2. Students need to master standard English for upward mobility.	Females	Males	.03
	White	POC	.01
	41–60 yrs. old	21–40	.03
	Bachelor's	Doctorate	.000
	NCTE	CCCC	.000
	15 yrs. teaching	1–6 yrs.	.02
	HS	Univ.	.000
3. In the home, students should be exposed to standard English only.	White	POC	.01
	Bachelor's	Doctorate	.000
	NCTE	CCCC	.000
	HS	Univ.	.000
4. Students who use nonstandard dialects should be taught in standard English.	White	POC	.001
	60+ yrs. old	21–40	.002
	Bachelor's	Doctorate	.000
	NCTE	CCCC	.000
	1–14 yrs. teaching	15 yrs.	.001
	HS	Univ.	.000

Table 2.2. *Continued*

Statement	Tend to Agree	Tend to Disagree	Sig.
5. There are valid reasons for using nonstandard dialects.	Males	Females	.008
	POC	White	.000
	21–40 yrs. old	60+	.01
	CCCC	NCTE	.000
	Community college (CC) & Univ.	HS	.000
	Doctorate	Bachelor's	.000
6. There are valid reasons for using languages other than English.	Males	Females	.04
	POC	White	.007
	Doctorate	Bachelor's and master's	.000
	CCCC	NCTE	.000
	Univ. and CC	HS	.000
7. Students should learn grammar rules to improve their ability to understand and communicate concepts and information.	Bachelor's	Doctorate	.000
	NCTE	CCCC	.000
	HS	Univ.	.000

Note: Statistically significant at .05 or lower.

strategically, even if at times unconsciously, privilege certain cultural practices and languages. Furthermore, critical language and literacy theorists (Fairclough, Gee, Rampton, Canagarajah, Heath, Lee, Giroux, Villanueva), multicultural education scholars (Banks, Delpit, Ladson-Billings, Sleeter), linguists (Labov, Kachru, Rickford, Smitherman), and bilingual education scholars (Cummins, Crawford, Faltis, Hakuta and Snow, Krashen, Macedo) have long argued that incorporating the language practices of language minority groups into their formal education is ethical and promotes sociocognitive development and academic achievement. Yet roughly one-third of our professional organization does not appear to be in accordance with these policies and principles. This might be due to the dominance of the ideology of English monolingualism in America, the belief that it is not normal for citizens to be bilingual or multilingual and that once one learns English, it should be spoken all the time, given the superpower status of English worldwide (Shannon). Such a view is shortsighted.

Within a global scheme, even the idea of World English is misguided, insofar as there are many Englishes, so that those who already have skills in more than one language are those who are more prepared to enter a global market than those who are confined to a single variety of a single language.[2] What we refer to as "English" in the United States is something different in Britain, in Zimbabwe, in Japan, or in India, for example (see Cliett in this volume for a fuller discussion of World Englishes).

I suspect that members of our profession who espouse the ideology of monolingualism do so because they view English as the carrier of cultural and economic capital, and they believe that it is in the best interest of students to know it, if nothing else. Another reason that many language educators may support the ideology of English monolingualism is that they may see themselves as guiding school-age adolescents or traditional college students (young adults) into financially secure and more profitable areas of the labor market (the "American dream factor"). As discussed by Horner and Trimbur, however, this view is contradictory, as both those for and against English Only use this assumption in their arguments. Those for English Only legislation cite the "American dream factor," saying that the English language is needed to achieve the American dream. This is a very popular American myth. On the other hand, those against English Only cite the "American dream factor" when seeking increased funding for ESL classrooms.

Another possible explanation for the preference for English Only classrooms among one-third of the respondents in this study is that many educators may be concerned about the lack of one-to-one transfer of ideas in various languages. In this view, communication and social meaning are not the same in students' native languages, causing students not to grasp the conventional English meaning of an idea or concept (Widdowson). Educators may deem English monolingualism as more effective for student learning. Yet restricting languages other than English from the classroom limits access to literacy by limiting students' ability to construct meaning and knowledge from other discourse, culture, and language communities of which they may be a part.

While statement 2 could have been understood as gleaning attitudes about North American–born students who have acquired nonstandard varieties of English or nonstandard varieties of ESL, our hope was that it would also get at attitudes toward ESL learned abroad. In either case, multidialectal or multilingual students may acquire varieties of English very different from middle-class White students who may acquire standardized varieties in the home.

With regard to statement 2—"Students need to master standard English for upward mobility"—96.1 percent of members agreed with this statement and 3.9 percent disagreed. At first glance, this finding seems unproblematic, since one of the charges of the language educator is to help students use standardized English as a tool for personal empowerment (see tables 2.2 and 2.3). Table 2.3 shows the data with regard to statistically significant correlations.

Respondents in the 41–60 age range tended to agree more than did those professionals in the 21–40 age group. I'd like to focus on the age-graded difference concerning the value of standardized English for careers and occupations. I wonder if the more mature members of our organizations lost their optimism for the equitable society that they worked for in the 1960s. On the other hand, will this trend continue? That is, will those in the younger category become less optimistic or conservative with age on this particular issue? It could be that with experience, those who will have been teaching longer will realize that upward mobility involves much more than the acquisition of language mastery. It could be argued just as well that the privilege of white skin, among other factors, plays a role in determining upward mobility. I think it is also important to note that more females than males agreed with the idea of standardized English for upward mobility. It has long been thought that females use more standardized forms than males.

Statements 3, 4, and 5 sought to get at attitudes regarding nonstandard varieties of English or "dialects." A large percentage, 86.8,

Table 2.3. Significant Demographic Categories by Agreement and Disagreement with Statement 2

Tend to Agree	Tend to Disagree	Sig.
Female	Male	.03
White	POC	.01
41–60 yrs. old	21–40 yrs. old	.03
Bachelor's	Doctorate	.000
NCTE	CCCC	.000
15 yrs. teaching	1–6 yrs. teaching	.02
HS	Univ.	.000

Note: Statistically significant at .05 or lower.

Table 2.4. Significant Demographic Categories by Agreement and Disagreement with Statement 3

Tend to Agree	Tend to Disagree	Sig.
White	POC	.01
Bachelor's	Doctorate	.000
NCTE	CCCC	.000
HS	Univ.	.000

Note: Statistically significant at .05 or lower.

disagreed with statement 3, "In the home, students should be exposed to standard English only," while 13.2 percent agreed with it. Those in agreement tended to be White high school teachers; those who disagreed were, significantly, university professors of Color (see tables 2.2 and 2.4).

An overwhelming 89.5 percent agreed with statement 4, "Students who use nonstandard dialects should be taught in standard English," while 10.5 percent disagreed. Table 2.5 shows the demographic breakdown of respondents in terms of significant agreement and disagreement on this statement (see table 2.2 also).

Responses to this statement break down along racial lines with Whites agreeing significantly more than people of Color. The age-graded difference is interesting. Educators over 60 years old agree significantly more than educators in the 21–40 age group. People with bachelor's degrees agree significantly more than those with

Table 2.5. Significant Demographic Categories by Agreement
and Disagreement with Statement 4

Tend to Agree	Tend to Disagree	Sig.
White	POC	.001
60+ yrs. old	21–40 yrs. old	.002
Bachelor's	Doctorate	.000
NCTE	CCCC	.000
1–14 yrs. teaching	15+ yrs. teaching	.001
HS	Univ.	.000

Note: Statistically significant at .05 or lower.

doctorates. NCTE members agree more than CCCC members, and
high school teachers agree more than college professors. What does
seem odd is that those teaching fewer years—1–14—agree significantly more than those teaching 15 years or more. This doesn't jibe
with the finding that those 60 and over agreed more. This leads me
to speculate that those respondents in the 60-plus category did not
necessarily teach 15 years or more, since those who taught longer
tended to disagree with this statement.

It is interesting to juxtapose responses to statements 3 and 4
against responses to statement 1. Recall that roughly two-thirds of
the respondents supported the use of languages other than English
in the classroom, and they tended to be university professors of
Color. Several inferences can be drawn from these data. It appears
that language and dialect are not equally valued. Generally, in this
study, White high school teachers value second languages more
than what they view as nonstandard dialects in the classroom. This
view, however, is uncritical because it reproduces rather than questions relations between dominant and subordinate groups in society.
James Milroy's discussion of the "consequences of standardisation"
sheds light on the importance of examining ideologies, which inform language policies and attitudes toward language use:

> In debates about language use and language teaching, lan-
> guage experts seem often to have played into the hands of
> those who support narrowly "correct" usage by giving too

little attention to the fact that what is involved is only superficially a debate about language and is more fundamentally a debate about ideologies. (23)

Ideologies that follow from and support people in positions of power, wealth, and status, consciously or unconsciously, uphold systems of inequity. Arguments such as "students need access to the mainstream" and "students need access to standardized varieties of English" do more to uphold the idea of a monolithic "correct" English and the system that it supports than they do to benefit the subordinated, stigmatized, or least preferred social groups.

The differing responses to statements 5, "There are valid reasons for using nonstandard dialects," and 6, "There are valid reasons for using languages other than English," are also revealing. Only 7.4 percent believed that there are no valid reasons for using other languages; however, more than twice as many, nearly 20 percent of the respondents, did not believe there were valid reasons for using nonstandard dialects. Stated differently, only 80 percent of respondents espouse ideologies of bi/multilingualism as far as nonstandard language varieties are concerned. Significantly, more males, people of Color, and university and community college professors agreed that "there are valid reasons for using languages other than English" than did females, Whites, and high school teachers.

Statement 7 reads: "Students should learn grammar rules to improve their ability to understand and communicate concepts and information." Over three-fourths, or 78.4 percent, of educators agreed, while 21.6 percent disagreed (see tables 2.2 and 2.6).

This statement was designed to get at instructors' thinking about the utility of teaching grammar as rules that represent one-to-one correspondences between referents and their symbolic representation and interpretation. I think it is interesting that this statement did not break down along the lines of race, gender, or age. Rather, the tendency was that high school teachers and university professors responded to the statement differently. It is safe to say that there are beliefs and schools of thought among college teachers that are not held by high school teachers. Some of these differences are

Table 2.6. Significant Demographic Categories by Agreement and Disagreement with Statement 7

Tend to Agree	Tend to Disagree	Sig.
Bachelor's	Doctorate	.000
NCTE	CCCC	.000
HS	Univ.	.000

Note: Statistically significant at .05 or lower.

no doubt related to training. I am hesitant to speculate beyond this point, since it is difficult to be sure of the pedagogical contexts that those in agreement with the statement had in mind. To look at it from the perspective of those who answered affirmatively, it is true that understanding sentence-level standardized grammar rules can help one to discern a one-dimensional level of meaning, but grammar is probably best investigated in the context of discourse to move students to critical language awareness and the multiple possibilities for meaning. From a critical perspective, then, students should be led to investigate grammatical rules as choices for specific rhetorical purposes.

Training in Concepts of Language and Language Diversity

The survey was also concerned with academic training in language diversity. Based on the pilot survey data, a list of the most common college courses in language was compiled. We defined "training" as completion of these particular college courses: African American English, American Dialects, Introduction to the English Language, and Linguistics for Teachers. We defined "no training" as having had none of the aforementioned courses. There was no statistically significant difference between training in language and any of the seven demographic groups in the survey: race, age, gender, educational level, membership in CCCC or NCTE, and number of years of teaching. In fact, nearly one-third of all demographic groups had had no college course in language. Yet training in language and language diversity was recognized as necessary for anyone preparing to be a language arts teacher today.

The study's prediction was that those who had themselves undergone such training would be more likely to recommend training for others, but there was no statistically significant difference between those who had had training and those who had none. Over a fourth of the respondents had had no course in language diversity in college, yet 95.5 percent agreed that such a course was necessary for teacher preparation today. Both groups recognized the need for such training, and both groups overwhelmingly recommended that those in language arts teacher preparation programs today take a course in language. What this says to me is that most of the profession realizes that training in language diversity is an important requirement and may enhance their teaching.

Respondents were asked to rank the recommended courses in order of importance. The courses were ranked as follows (the lower the mean score, the higher, or more important, the ranking):

Introduction to the English Language 1.60
Linguistics for Teachers 2.04
American Dialects 2.42
African American English 3.49

Since one goal of the study was concerned with the type of training in language diversity necessary to prepare language arts teachers, it is worth examining this aspect of the survey's results in greater detail. Statistical significance was found in terms of responses to statements 1, 3, 4, 5, and 6.

Significantly, more language educators, 34.8 percent, who had taken an African American English (AAE) course strongly disagreed with statement 1 than those who had not taken an AAE course and who strongly disagreed, 18.7 percent (sig. 007*). (See Language Policy Committee 20.)

A similar pattern appears with responses to statement 3. Again, AAE proved statistically significant in terms of responses to this statement. None—not one—of those who had taken an African American English course strongly agreed with this statement, and 49.2 percent of this group strongly disagreed, whereas only 32.1 percent strongly disagreed among those who had not taken African American English (sig. 01*). (See Language Policy Committee 20.)

Those educators who had taken both African American English and American Dialects responded in significantly different ways to statement 4 from those who had taken Introduction to the English Language and Linguistics for Teachers. Of those who took a course in African American English, 7.6 percent strongly disagreed with the statement "Students who use nonstandard dialects should be taught in standard English," compared with only 1.8 percent of those who had not taken a course in African American English. In the case of the American Dialects course group, 5.1 percent strongly disagreed with the statement, compared with only 1.6 percent among those who had not taken an American Dialects course.

Again, both the African American English and the American Dialects (AD) course groups differed significantly from the Introduction to the English Language and Linguistics for Teachers course groups with respect to statement 5. Significantly, more of the AAE course group strongly agreed with the statement (49.3 percent) than those in the non-AAE course group (24.3 percent). Furthermore, among the AAE course group, none—not one—strongly disagreed with the statement, compared to 6.7 percent of the non-AAE group. Among those who did not have an AD course, the percentage of those disagreeing with the statement (14.9 percent) was twice that of those who took an AD course (7.1 percent).

Among those who took AAE, 62.7 percent agreed with statement 6. Only 39.1 percent agreed among those who did not take AAE, while none of the AAE course group strongly disagreed. Results seem to suggest that research and information on dialect/language variation and bi/multilingualism are being conveyed in courses dealing with African American English and American Dialects, and this information has had an impact on some language arts teachers who have taken such courses. However, the same knowledge and impact were not found among those language arts professionals who took Introduction to the English Language and Linguistics for Teachers courses.

Members' Descriptions of Their Own Language Use

Four categories for describing respondents' language now and in the past were derived from the pilot study. These were: multilingual, multidialectal, Standard American English most of the time, and nonstandard American English. Comparisons were made within demographic groups to ascertain which particular group within a demographic set tended to select a category more than another group within that set. Using this kind of comparison, several statistically significant results were found.

Language now multilingual: people of Color (POC), doctorates.

Language now multidialectal: POC; males; doctorates; CCCC members; university teachers.

Language now Standard American English most of the time: Whites; respondents 41–60 years old; bachelor's degrees; NCTE members; high school teachers; respondents teaching 15-plus years.

Language now nonstandard American English: POC.

Past language multilingual: POC; community college teachers.

Past language multidialectal: males; POC; holders of doctorates; CCCC members; university teachers.

Past language Standard American English most of the time: Whites; respondents 60-plus years old; bachelor's degrees; NCTE members; respondents teaching 15-plus years; high school teachers.

Past language nonstandard American English: males; POC.

These results show a general pattern that educators of Color (POC) identify their language use in the present and past as multilingual and multidialectal, including the use of nonstandard varieties of American English. We can be reasonably certain that educators of Color know and use standardized English, but they understand themselves to use it in specific contexts as opposed to most of the time, and they are multilingual and multidialectal. Generally, male educators and educators of Color were the only groups to describe their past language use as nonstandardized varieties of American English. Another general pattern that emerges is that Ph.D.'s tended to describe their language along the same lines as people of Color. Generally, White educators described their language use in the present and past as Standard American English most of the time. This group tends to be members of NCTE, bachelor's degree holders, high school teachers, and teachers for more than 15 years.

Knowledge of and Support for CCCC/NCTE Language Policies

The survey sought to uncover the membership's knowledge of and support for the CCCC/NCTE language policies "Students' Right to Their Own Language" and the National Language Policy. About two-thirds of the members of NCTE and CCCC as represented in this sample were not familiar with these two organizational policies. The difference between those who had no knowledge of the two organizational language policies and those who were familiar with the policies can be accounted for in terms of the seven demographic characteristics, all of which proved to be statistically significant. These results parallel findings in other areas of the survey relative to differences in response between demographic groups. Generally, people of Color tended to be more familiar with "Students' Right" and "English Plus," a recommendation within the National Language Policy, than Whites (see table 2.7); respondents with doctorates more familiar than those with bachelor's degrees; members of CCCC more familiar than NCTE members; university teachers more familiar than high school teachers; males generally more familiar than females. Those who had been teaching fifteen years or more were more likely to have knowledge of the policies than those who had been teaching 1–6 years. In terms of age, the trend was that the older the member, the greater the likelihood of familiarity with the policies. (However, the same does not hold true in terms of support or opposition to the policies.)

While language educators of Color are divided surprisingly equally among those who are familiar with both organizational policies and those who are not, slightly favoring the knowledgeable, over twice as many White language educators are unfamiliar with both policies. Perhaps the knowledge of these policies among language educators of Color can be attributed in part to vested interest and personal experience with the issues, revealing the importance of cultural experiences in knowledge making. This is not to say that White language educators have no interest or experience in these issues. Clearly, they do. However, the principles, ideas, and practices represented by these policies should be known throughout the profession.

Of those educators who were familiar with the two policies—some 35 percent in each case—there was considerably more support for English Plus than for "Students' Right" (82.3 percent and 67.9 percent, respectively). In great measure, this may be attributable to the tremendous controversy stemming from passage of the "Students' Right" resolution a generation ago, a language policy formulated during the tumultuous social changes of the 1960s and 1970s. I am reminded by Bruch and Marback that many teachers who know of "Students' Right" resolution interpret it to mean that they are obligated to promote standardized English in public official spaces and teach the appropriateness of other language varieties in the home or community settings. If Bruch and Marback are correct, this explains why many would feel it unnecessary to implement linguistically diverse teaching methods in their curricula. By contrast, there was little opposition to the English Plus policy passed in 1988. The discrepancy between levels of support of the two policies in the 1990s may also be attributed to lack of practical preparation, that is, in the case of "Students' Right," preparation for including various nonstandard dialects as a central aspect of the classroom language education experience. As for English Plus, perhaps the sentiment is that there is less concern about practical implementation of language activities since ESL teachers, not general language arts educators, will be responsible for teaching second language speakers.

Pedagogical Approaches to Language Diversity

Another area that the survey sought to uncover was the membership's teaching practices with regard to language diversity in speech and writing. Virtually all the respondents indicated that they dis-

Table 2.7. Familiarity with "Students' Right to Their Own Language" and "English Plus" by Demographic Group

Characteristic	Familiar with "Students' Right"			Familiar with "English Plus"		
	Yes	No	Sig.	Yes	No	Sig.
Race						
POC	51.1	48.9	.000	54.9	45.1	.000
White	31.9	68.1		30.0	70.0	
Educational level						
Bachelor's	16.5	83.5	.000	25.0	75.0	.000
Master's	24.4	75.9		27.5	72.5	
Doctorate	59.3	40.7		48.1	51.9	
Membership						
NCTE	20.7	79.3	.000	27.7	72.3	.000
CCCC	58.4	41.6		44.4	55.6	
Teaching level						
High school	16.5	83.5	.000	24.4	75.6	.000
Community college	44.4	55.6		37.7	62.3	
University	61.5	38.5		47.6	52.4	
Gender						
Female	30.3	69.7	.000	Not significant		
Male	48.5	51.5				
Age						
21–40	23.8	76.2	.000	Near significance at .066; trend for older respondents to be more familiar with the policies.		
41–60	36.9	63.1				
60+	48.5	51.5				
Years teaching						
1–6	23.2	76.8	.000	Near significance at .059; trend for respondents who have been teaching longer to be more familiar with the policies.		
7–14	28.1	71.9				
15+	39.1	60.9				

Note: Statistically significant at .05 or lower.

cuss language diversity, at least to some extent, with their students. Only 4.8 percent do not engage in any such discussions.

Respondents use a variety of approaches to discuss language diversity: readings on language matters, analysis of language use in literature and other creative forms, affirmations by the teacher that all languages and language varieties are equal. An overwhelming majority of members (82.4 percent) say their students raise issues and topics about language diversity. The students' concerns include differences between dialect and language, differences between dialect and slang, differences in the ways people speak, status and appropriateness of languages, and language varieties other than standardized English.

To get at the kinds of approaches that educators use with nonstandardized English speakers, the survey posed the question (to which multiple responses were allowed), What approaches do you use with students who use nonstandard dialect features in their speech?

44.4% correct students' writing, not their speech
13.0% tell students that for an English class, only standard English is appropriate
100% use private conferences to discuss issues of correctness
24% might say nothing
82.4% discuss the importance of knowing both standard and nonstandard English and the contexts of appropriate use for each

In terms of the same question applied to students who use nonstandard dialect features in their writing, members gave the following responses (again, multiple responses were allowed):

19.9% instruct students that for an English class, only standard English is appropriate in writing
53.4% use private conferences
84.3% discuss the importance of standard and nonstandard English and contexts of appropriate use for each
11.2% might say nothing

It is interesting to note the difference between the strategies used for speech and those used for writing. The most striking is that 100 percent of respondents used private conferences to discuss matters of oral speech variation, whereas only 53.4 percent used private conferences for written language variation. In spoken or written contexts, though, there is still a significant percentage of educators who do not value nonstandard language variation in the classroom setting.

A Clear Need for Further Training of English Teachers

The data from this study show that, overall, we language educators have a complex mix of attitudes about not only our students' language but also our own, which is influenced, in part, by race, classes or training, gender, where we teach, how long we've taught, and our ages. Overwhelmingly in this study, educators of Color supported the maintenance of diverse dialects and languages in the classroom more than White language educators. Our data also show that Whites identified themselves as standardized English speakers most of the time in the past and present, as opposed to educators of Color, who identified their language use as multilingual or multidialectal, including present nonstandardized usage. These findings taken together imply that some White instructors need more meaningful experiences with linguistically diverse speakers in their everyday lives. More facility is needed with nonstandardized dialects. This may account for the reason that more White instructors did not support the usage of nonstandardized dialects and languages other than English in the classroom as much as educators of Color did. Although most of the language educators surveyed want to foster language diversity, some don't feel they have the training to provide it. Our data also revealed that classes such as African American English and American Dialects proved significant in distinguishing those teachers knowledgeable and open to language diversity in the classroom from those who were not.

Significantly, the majority of those surveyed, while believing in the need for training in linguistic diversity, were unaware of the published positions of their professional organizations, namely the 1974 resolution, "Students' Right to Their Own Language," and the 1988 "National Language Policy." Those who were aware could be distinguished along the lines of race, education, teaching level, and organizational affiliation. The survey also revealed a split between high school teachers and college/university teachers on a several issues.

We can see a rich array of variables and issues that deserve deeper reflection as we consider what we as a profession can do to improve the delivery of services to the diverse students (including White ones) who enter our classes. "The Language Knowledge and Awareness Survey Final Research Report," available through the CCCC website, contains a list of recommendations. Those recommendations could be summed up in this way: Our theories and practices must keep pace with the diversity in our classrooms, with research, and with social change.

I began this essay by discussing the rhetorical training of Justice Clarence Thomas. Nurtured in this society and its classrooms, Thomas was indoctrinated into the ideology of English monolingualism and monodialectalism. He was taught to devalue the Black cultural aspects of his identity, including his language use and the voices that struggled to create a space for his on the Supreme Court. By virtue of his status, some would consider him a success, although he is not known for progressive thinking or action. Our profession must continue to struggle against traditional concepts of literacy education and remain observant that literacy education is always political, subjective, and ever shifting according to societal needs. Right now, we have a surplus of Clarence Thomases.

Notes

All data are reported from the *Language Knowledge and Awareness Survey* final research report, submitted by the CCCC Language Policy Committee to NCTE, January 2000, available on-line at http://www.ncte.org/cccc/langsurvey.pdf.

1. See, for example, Williams, *Language and Poverty* and "Psychological Correlates," and Williams and Whitehead.

2. See Warschauer for a helpful discussion of global economy and the future of English teaching.

Works Cited

Banks, James. *Teaching Strategies For Ethnic Studies*. Boston: Allyn, 1991.
Bowie, Carole. "Influencing Future Teachers' Attitudes Toward Black English:

Are We Making a Difference?" *Journal of Teacher Education* 3.1 (1994): 112–18.

Bruch, Patrick, and Richard Marback. "Race, Literacy, and the Value of Rights Rhetoric in Composition Studies." *CCC* 53 (2002): 651–74.

Byrnes, Deborah A., and Gary Kiger. "Language Attitudes of Teachers Scale (LATS)." *Educational and Psychological Measurement* 54.1 (1994): 227–31.

———. "Teachers Attitudes about Language Differences." 1991. ERIC Document ED340232.

Canagarajah, A. Suresh. *Resisting Linguistic Imperialism in English Teaching.* Oxford: Oxford UP, 1999.

CCCC Language Policy Committee. *Language Knowledge and Awareness Survey.* Final Report (corrected copy). Jan. 2000 <http://www.ncte.org/cccc/langsurvey.pdf>.

Crawford, James. *Hold Your Tongue: Bilingualism and the Politics of English Only.* Reading, MA: Addison-Wesley, 1992.

Cummins, James. *Bilingualism and Minority-Language Children.* Toronto: Ontario Institute for Studies in Education, 1981.

Delpit, Lisa. *Other People's Children: Cultural Conflict in the Classroom.* New York: New, 1995.

Edelsky, Carole. *With Literacy and Justice for All: Rethinking the Social in Language and Education.* New York: Falmer, 1991.

Fairclough, Norman. *Critical Discourse Analysis: The Critical Study of Language.* London: Longman, 1995.

Faltis, Christine. "Bilingual Education in the United States." *Encyclopedia of Language and Education.* Ed. Jim Cummins and D. Lorsen. Dordrecht, the Netherlands: Kluwer·Academic, 1997. 189–97.

Fine, Michelle. "Silencing and Literacy." *Literacy among African American Youth: Issues in Learning, Teaching, and Schooling.* Ed. Vivian Gadsden and Daniel A. Wagner. Cresskill, NJ: Hampton P, 1995. 201–22.

Fordham, Signithia. *Blacked Out: Dilemmas of Race, Identity, and Success at Capital High.* Chicago: U of Chicago P, 1996.

———. "Racelessness as a Factor in Black Students' School Success: Pragmatic Strategy or Pyrrhic Victory?" *Harvard Educational Review* 58.1 (1988): 54–84.

Gee, James. *Social Linguistics and Literacies: Ideology in Discourses.* London: Taylor, 1996.

Gere, Anne R., and Eugene Smith. *Attitudes, Language, and Change.* Urbana, IL: NCTE, 1979.

Gilyard, Keith. *Voices of the Self.* Detroit: Wayne State UP, 1991.

Giroux, Henry. "Introduction: Literacy, Difference, and the Politics of Border Crossing." *Rewriting Literacy: Culture and Discourse of the Other.* Ed. Candace Mitchell and Kathleen Weiler. New York: Bergin, 1991. ix–xvi.

Hakuta, Kenji, and Catherine Snow. "The Role of Research in Policy Decisions about Bilingual Education." *NABE News* 9.3 (Spring) 1986: 1, 18–21.

Heath, Shirley Brice. *Ways with Words*. Cambridge: Cambridge UP, 1983.

Horner, Bruce, and John Trimbur. "English Only and U.S. College Composition." *CCC* 53 (2002): 594–630.

Kachru, Yamuna. "Cultural Meaning and Contrastive Rhetoric in English Education." *World Englishes* 16.3 (1997): 337–50.

Krashen, Stephen. *Under Attack: The Case Against Bilingual Education*. Culver City, CA: Language Education Assn., 1996.

Labov, William. "Can Reading Failure Be Reversed? A Linguistic Approach to the Question." *Literacy among African American Youth: Issues in Learning, Teaching, and Schooling*. Ed. Vivian Gadsden and Daniel A. Wagner. Cresskill, NJ: Hampton, 1995. 39–68.

Ladson-Billings, Gloria. "Toward a Theory of Culturally Relevant Pedagogy." *American Educational Research Journal* 32.3 (1995): 465–91.

Lambert, Wallace E., et al. "Evaluational Reactions to Spoken Language." *Journal of Abnormal and Social Psychology* 60.1 (1960): 44–51.

Lee, Carol D. *Signifying as a Scaffold to Literary Interpretation: The Pedagogical Implications of an African American Discourse Genre*. Urbana, IL: NCTE, 1993.

Lewis, Neil A. "The 43rd President: The Justice; Justice Thomas Speaks Out on a Timely Topic, Several of Them, in Fact." *New York Times* Online Archives 14 December 2000.

Macedo, Donaldo. *Literacies of Power: What Americans Are Not Allowed to Know*. Boulder: Westview, 1994.

Milroy, James. "Standardisation in Descriptive Linguistics." *Standard English: The Widening Debate*. Ed. Tony Bex and Richard Watts. New York: Routledge, 1999. 16–39.

Ogbu, John. "Adaptation to Minority Status and Impact on School Success." *Theory into Practice* 31.4 (1992): 287–95.

Rampton, Ben. "Retuning in Applied Linguistics." *International Journal of Applied Linguistics* 7.1 (1997): 3–25.

Rickford, John. *African American Vernacular English: Features, Evolution, Educational Implications*. Malden, MA: Blackwell, 1999.

Shannon, Sheila. "The Debate on Bilingual Education in the U.S.: Language Ideology as Reflected in the Practice of Bilingual Teachers." *Language Ideological Debates*. Ed. Jan Blommaert. Berlin: Mouton, 1999. 171–99.

Sledd, James. "Bidialectalism: The Linguistics of White Supremacy." *English Journal* 58.9 (1969): 1307–15.

Sleeter, Christine. Introduction. *Dancing with Bigotry: Beyond the Politics of Tolerance*. By Donald Macedo and Lilia I. Bartolome. New York: St. Martin's, 1999. vii–xv.

Smitherman, Geneva. "'Students' Right to Their Own Language': A Retrospective." *English Journal* 84.1 (1995): 21–27.

Steele, Claude. "Race and the Schooling of Black Americans." *Atlantic Monthly* 269.4 (1992): 68–78.

Taylor, Orlando. "Teachers' Attitudes Toward Black and Nonstandard English as Measured by the Language Attitude Scale." *Language Attitudes: Current Trends and Prospects.* Ed. Roger Shuy and Ralph Fasold. Washington, DC: Georgetown UP, 1973. 174–201.

Villanueva, Victor. *Bootstraps: From an American Academic of Color.* Urbana, IL: NCTE, 1993.

Warschauer, Mark. "The Changing Global Economy and the Future of English Teaching." *TESOL Quarterly* 34.3 (2000): 511–35.

Widdowson, Henry George. "Communication, Community, and the Problem of Appropriate Use." *Georgetown University Roundtable on Languages and Linguistics* (1992): 305–15.

Williams, Frederick, ed. *Language and Poverty: Perspectives on a Theme.* Chicago: Markham, 1970.

———. "Psychological Correlates of Speech Characteristics: On Sounding Disadvantaged." *Journal of Speech and Hearing Research* 13 (1970): 472–88.

Williams, Frederick, and Jack Whitehead. "Language in the Classroom: Studies of the Pygmalion Effect." *Language, Society, and Education.* Ed. Johanna S. DeStefano. Worthington, OH: Jones, 1973. 169–76.

3 / The Expanding Frontier of World Englishes
A New Perspective for Teachers of English
Victoria Cliett

English teachers have the opportunity to expand on new pedagogies in the face of the changing global landscape. The first frontier of global expansion is negative attitudes toward languages other than English and varieties other than "standard." In the future, English teachers will not be able to avoid the national issue of language rights. So we must educate ourselves about language diversity in this country and around the world. We will have to mediate national policy as schools face increasing pressure to prepare all students for democratic participation as citizens. To focus on a solely domestic concept of "standard English" would be to teachers' disadvantage in the changing cultural and global landscape. We will all have to deal with World Englishes. Thus, the concept of "standard English" is more complex than the English teacher's traditional notion of "correct" and "incorrect" language. The challenge to language scholars is to delineate how standard English is codified in different global contexts.

Ryuko Kubota and Lori Ward define the term "World Englishes" (WE) in relationship to the great diversity of varieties of standard English around the globe (Kubota and Ward). The concept of WE dates to the early 1960s, although there was no forum to discuss the international development of English until 1978 (Kachru). At that time, two organizations held conferences three months apart to discuss international and intranational developments in English: the East-West Culture Learning Institute in Honolulu, Hawai'i, and the Linguistic Institute of the Linguistic Society of America, held on the University of Illinois-Urbana campus. Both conferences considered questions that addressed the sociolinguistic and political contexts of countries where English is nonnative, the retention of English after colonization, and the sociolinguistic and linguistic profiles of the several standard varieties of English.

The Honolulu conference produced a formal statement on behalf of conference participants that affirmed the need to continue inquiry into the development of English as an international language and that the relationship between "standard" and "International" English needed further discussion. The Honolulu conference also asserted that there was a distinction between international and intranational uses of English. "International" refers to the use of English around the world, though the label is inaccurate insofar as it assumes a use of English that is unproblematic in "acceptance, proficiency, functions, norms, and creativity" (Kachru 215). "Intranational" refers to the unique uses of English within a country, official versus unofficial languages and local varieties, for example. Furthermore, the Honolulu statement outlined new practices in research and methodologies that were "consistent with the identities and functions of World Englishes" (210).

The statements coming from the conferences convened at Urbana during this period are significant in a discussion of World Englishes because they reflect a movement toward a more contextual and cultural discussion of English beyond functional use: literatures, sociolinguistic profiles, and local varieties of English (Kachru 211). The goals of the Urbana conferences were discussed at a subsequent colloquium in Honolulu in 1986. Focus was on the "concept of the linguistic 'power' of English with a cross-cultural perspective"; the goal was to assemble data from various English-using countries for the "study of such 'power' in the domains of literature and the media (film and journalism)" (211). Participants at this colloquium also identified theoretical and research areas for countries where English is not the native language; for example, in-depth studies on the national uses of English, identifying the main characteristics of English as it is used on international levels, comparing various contexts and methods of teaching in different cultural settings, and supporting classroom and literary critical study of literatures of English around the world (211).

Kachru has categorized World Englishes into three basic groupings, depending on the linguistic history of a particular country: (1) an Inner Circle, referring to countries where English is the mother tongue; (2) an Outer Circle, denoting countries where English is an additional, institutionalized language; and (3) an Expanding Circle, consisting of countries where English is a foreign language (213). The Inner Circle would include the United Kingdom, the United States, Canada, Ireland, New Zealand, and Australia. The Outer Circle includes former and current British and American colonies such as Bangladesh, Ghana, India, Malaysia, the Philippines, Sri Lanka, Tanzania, Zambia, Zimbabwe, Puerto Rico, the U.S. Virgin Islands, and other Caribbean countries. The Expanding Circle includes China, Egypt, Indonesia, Israel, Japan, Korea, Nepal, Russia, Saudi Arabia, Taiwan, and various South American countries.

Anne Pakir asserts that the "flourishing of world Englishes naturally leads to the idea of standards and codification . . . with a move to saleability in the linguistic marketplace" (171). However, the process of codifying standard English is far from simple. Owners of English in the Outer Circle are "players" of English in the Inner Circle, making and introducing their own rules. In the Outer Circle, English has "plurocentricity" rather than "duo-centricity," that is, British and American English no longer reign as the centers of language variation and change. As John Norris indicates, it is unrealistic to expect that Inner Circle countries can claim sole ownership of English. In fact, citizens of Australia may eventually consider their language "Australian," for instance, and Americans may come to think of theirs as "American" rather than "English." The lesson to be learned in the United States is that what teachers perceive as "nonstandard" English plays a significant role in daily language use around the globe.

According to Pakir and other scholars, the commercial value of English as a spoken language has cemented its widespread global use. In Singapore, for example, the national airport employs electronic signboards in English as well as Chinese, Malay, Tamil, Bahasa, Indonesia, Thai, Bangladeshi, and the Myanmar language (Pakir 170). Singapore also uses English in street signs and for public information. However, the huge influx of international workers and visitors who bring economic capital required Singapore to accommodate alternatives to standard English (171).

The economic and cultural capital of English opens the door for varieties other than standard to become accepted through the codification process. Of course, with standardization comes reduced tolerance of language varieties. Pakir identifies five primary problems with codification:

1. Prescriptivism vs. descriptivism: the codification of World Englishes does not necessarily happen before or after standardization; the codification of World English is contextual.
2. Choice of standards: conflicts between external and internal English language practices in a country.
3. Participatory vs. separatist: should there be mutual collaboration or "us" vs. "them"?
4. Content of standards: tailoring the codification of the language to represent the "distinctive cultural identity" of the native population.
5. Acceptance of standards: approval of the codified language by professionals, the population, and institutions (175–76).

Yet in a country such as Singapore, there exists several legitimate reasons for the codification of its English (called "SingE"). This codified variety could be used in schools as an appropriate model for the teaching and learning of English, thereby bridging the gap between children who speak English and teachers whose first language is not English but who must nevertheless teach in English. As well, SingE can be used to demonstrate a "prevention" against the "degeneration" of this variety of English so as to lend it an international status (Pakir 177). In many countries outside the Inner Circle, English is encouraged in and outside of the classroom (although not in the home). The classroom is not the sole influence on language use, as too many U.S. teachers seem to assume. In Outer and Expanding Circle countries, English language use is negotiated and relearned frequently outside of the classroom, and new varieties emerge from the seemingly insignificant interactions of everyday life. Furthermore, while the political and cultural climate concerning language varieties in the United States has often been turbulent, in other countries, consideration of national language diversity has become imperative in the political arena.

South Africa is a case in point. South Africa has undergone many changes in the last few years, including winning independence from apartheid and from European colonialism. With the new political changes, South Africa has restructured its language use. In the past, South Africa's linguistic diversity was used for a "divide-and-rule" strategy by the White ruling elite (Smitherman). At the inception of apartheid, the African majority was divided into distinct groups, according to language, with indigenous languages devalued. However, since becoming a democracy, South Africa has adopted a policy of "English Plus" (while the United States continues to adopt policies of "English Only," despite—or because of—the huge constituency of linguistic minorities in the country). The new South Africa has adopted a constitutional provision that recognizes eleven official languages, with English being only one of the eleven. The constitution promotes multilingualism, prohibits the use of language to exploit and divide, and requires that all eleven languages be recognized equally in all areas of public administration. Of course, as Smitherman notes, it remains to be seen whether South Africa will be able to fully realize its constitutional "dream" of official multilingualism.

In the United States, English teachers must come to grips with the reality that linguistic diversity is here to stay and, in fact, will become even more widespread during this new century. For example, over the past decade, the population of citizens of Color, in particular, Blacks and Latinos, has increased significantly. According to the 2000 census, Black non-Hispanic citizens and those of Hispanic origin now combine to represent nearly 25 percent of the U.S. population. It is clear that language diversity will remain relevant in political and academic agendas of the twenty-first century.

What will English teachers do to accommodate these population changes? Given global linguistic diversity and the concomitant emergence of World Englishes, how will twenty-first-century language arts and composition teachers juggle the demands of cultural diversity and the pedagogical needs of the classroom? Now is the time for teacher education to change, to toss out the old ideas about a uniform, monolithic standard English. Teaching educators about global varieties of standard English can help educators design new theoretical and pedagogical models for the changing landscape of English.

Brown and Peterson conducted a study to assess the effect of knowledge about World Englishes on attitudes toward and perceptions about World Englishes and "nonnative" speakers of English. The "subjects" were students enrolled in a master's level program in Teaching English to Speakers of Other Languages (TESOL). The researchers compiled a list of twenty-seven concepts (for example, ideological concepts, concepts about varieties of English) utilized by scholars in discussions and analyses of the World English paradigm. These concepts formed the basis of judgments about World Englishes and their millions of speakers, including those whose first language is not English.

The student-subjects were divided into two groups and given different amounts of instruction in World English concepts. One group received only the TESOL program's four-hour introductory instructional module in World Englishes. The other group received the same introductory instruction plus an additional three-credit course in World Englishes, for a total of thirty-four hours of instructional time. The students who received more instructional time not only had developed a more complex knowledge base and more highly differentiated conceptual categories about the English language and its speakers but also displayed more sophisticated and complex classifications and descriptions about speakers of English. For example, whereas the four-hour instructional group of students classified English speakers into the simplistic dichotomy of "native-nonnative," the student group who had been exposed to more hours of instruction described English speakers in terms of sociolinguistic norms and language policies.

The concept of World Englishes allows for a variety of standard Englishes, many of which, as stated earlier, are comprised of forms and patterns that problematize the traditional notion of "nonstandard English" in the United States. In the face of this global recognition of language diversity, it is imperative that English teachers address the pedagogical and curricular changes that multilingual and multidialectal classrooms demand. To be sure, lack of exposure to the study of language variation has had a negative impact on teachers' attitudes and responses toward language diversity. As has been noted in Richardson's chapter in this volume, in the CCCC Language Policy Committee's survey of NCTE and CCCC members, 28.4 percent of the respondents had had no course in language diversity in their college training (although, encouragingly, 95.5 percent of the respondents agreed that such training was necessary for teacher education).

In pedagogy, there are several competing theories on the role English education should take, theories that have intersected with postcolonial and cultural studies. For the most part, most theorists in composition, World Englishes, and postcolonial theory agree that teachers of English, especially on the international front, will be intermediaries between the hegemonic and global standard English and the local and marginal varieties of English. Wimal Dissanayake asserts that any interrogation of World Englishes requires consideration of the global and the local. Writing produced by nonnative speakers of English is metaphorical in nature (137). Hence, the teaching of writing in standard English engages some reorientation of classroom knowledge that must serve the larger agenda of standard English.

Alastair Pennycook considers a liberal and conservative polarity in the international use of a standard English in asking if its dominance is the result of being imposed or its being accepted (73–74). Pennycook takes the position that critical pedagogy must dismantle language norms and discourses. The relationship of teacher and student in the standard English classroom can be problematized when considering that teachers can be foreigners to students in ways that do not necessarily follow nationalist discourse (302). One of the prominent gaps in English is that between a still male academy and the female teaching practitioner (303). Education by nature is political, so standard English cannot be considered the exception, the apolitical. The means of production that the teaching of English serves must be considered. The teaching of English must also be self-reflexive, never assuming that one particular worldview is capable of working in all classrooms (305).

For teachers of English, there are several implications that arise from global English expansion. New and innovative teaching strategies for a linguistically diverse population will need to be acquired. This multidimensional pedagogy will have to address the social and political history of English and other languages. Standard English will have to be taught as only one of several appropriate varieties, depending on context and situation. New media of learning will require acceptance and tolerance of new languages. Effective teaching encompasses a global, rather than a local, method of teaching. The teacher-training curriculum must include study and examination of language systems and teaching methods in other parts of the world.

The good news is that trends show that the new generation of college English teachers have opened themselves up to new language pedagogies and have expressed interest in workshops that will enable them to overcome language barriers in the classrooms. These new attitudes must become the standard in language arts instruction for the twenty-first century.

Works Cited

Brown, Kimberley, and Jay Peterson. "Exploring Conceptual Frameworks: Framing a World Englishes Paradigm." Smith and Forman 32–47.

CCCC Language Policy Committee. *Language Knowledge and Awareness Survey*. Final Report. Jan. 2000. 3 Mar. 2003 <http://www.ncte.org/cccc/langsurvey.pdf>.

Dissanayake, Wimal. "Cultural Studies and World Englishes: Some Topics for Further Exploration." Smith and Forman 126–45.

Kachru, Braj B. "World Englishes 2000: Resources for Research and Teaching." Smith and Forman 209–51.

Kubota, Ryuko, and Lori Ward. "Exploring Linguistic Diversity Through World Englishes." *English Journal* 89.6 (2000): 80–86.

Linguistic Society of America. *Statement on Language Rights.* June 1996. 3 Mar. 2003 <http://www.lsadc.org/langrite.html>.

Norris, John. "english or English? Attitudes, Local Varieties and English Language Teaching." *Teaching of English as a Second or Foreign Language (TESL-EJ)* 3.1 (1997). 12 Jan. 2001 <http://www-writing.berkeley.edu/TESL-EJ/ej09/a2.html>.

Pakir, Anne. "Standards and Codification for World Englishes." Smith and Forman 169–81.

Pennycook, Alastair. *The Cultural Politics of English as an International Language.* New York: Longman, 1994.

Smith, Larry E., and Michael L. Forman, eds. *World Englishes 2000.* Honolulu: U of Hawai'i P, 1997.

Smitherman, Geneva. "Language and Democracy in the United States of America and South Africa." *Language and Institutions in Africa.* Ed. Sinfree B. Makoni and Nkonko Kamwangamalu. Cape Town: Centre for Advanced Studies of African Society, 2000. 65–92.

Teachers of English to Speakers of Other Languages. *Policy Statement of the TESOL Board on Language Varieties.* Oct. 1996. 3 Mar. 2003 <http://www.tesol.org/assoc/statements/languagevarieties.html>.

4 / Language Diversity in Teacher Education and in the Classroom

Arnetha F. Ball and Rashidah Jaami` Muhammad

As we discussed issues of language diversity in our preservice teacher education classroom, one student read this statement from his Methods of Teaching English course journal: "'I be' is not acceptable, even on the streets." Echoing this student's sentiments, another preservice teacher noted that, for her, "double negatives are like scraping nails on a chalkboard." Still another student, who was only one semester away from student teaching, offered the following advice in a somewhat condescending tone: "We must tell our students that although it is okay and wonderful that they have and use their relaxed, less formal language in certain instances, it is important that they also have the skills and know-how to use Standard English." Yet another preservice teacher added the following comment to the mix of our classroom conversation.

> [I believe that] students will suffer personal consequences if they fail to respect and accept language diversity. However, I also believe that, for now in our society, people are not only judged by the color of their skin but also classified by the way that they speak. The richest, most intelligent and generous person in our country would be ridiculed if he/she did not speak Standard English.

Like the other statements made before this one, this student's comment reflects the dominant attitude expressed by most preservice teachers when the conversation arises concerning the too-often ignored issue of the presence of language diversity in our classrooms. While this student seems to be suggesting that speech patterns constitute a predominant determinant in students' lifelong social or economic success, perhaps the most serious pedagogical assertion comes from the student who shared the following thought:

> In today's society, grammar is often considered an indication of one's class and cultural background. I would not want my students to experience bias against them because I have not done my job properly—by omitting the teaching of how, when, and where they should speak standard language. I will explain to my students that many people believe that people who do not speak correctly will have little opportunity for advancement in our country. It's important that I teach my students to use proper pronunciation, vocabulary, and word usage. Every time my students give an oral presentation before their peers, I will expect them to speak using standard language. Also, whenever I assign my students a writing assignment, they will be expected to write their papers using standard English.

These comments expressed by our nation's future educators indicate that there may be very little tolerance for language variation and for the expression of ideas from diverse cultures in many of our nation's future classrooms. Unfortunately, it seems that—unless there is effective intervention that causes some change in these teachers' attitudes—"zero tolerance" will be the order of the day when it comes to language variation in these teachers' classrooms. It also appears that these future teachers have accepted the myth of an idealized "standard English" and only one "correct" way to express ideas.

In general, it appears that there are three interrelated misconceptions concerning the existence of standard and nonstandard English. One is that there is a uniform standard English that has been reduced to a set of consistent rules. Related to this myth is a second misconception: that these "correct," consistent rules should be followed by all American English speakers. The third is that this mythical standard English must be safeguarded by everyone connected with its use, particularly classroom teachers.

The notion that language can be "correct" or "incorrect" is a myth. In reality, language is dynamic and ever changing; consequently, there are no permanent or absolute standards. In fact, the notion of "good" and "bad" English is a misguided one. We can better evaluate linguistic systems by assessing whether or not a given system is the most appropriate or most effective variety of English for the particular communication at hand. From this perspective, a style that may be generally perceived of as nonstandard can be just as appropriate as one that is considered to be standard, depending on the demands of the particular communicative situation. Despite scholarly research on language over the past several decades, such misconceptions continue to be widely held by a large number of future teachers who are, or soon will be, entering our nation's classrooms. The comments from the preservice teachers in the class described above are, unfortunately, fairly typical. Reading these comments caused both of the authors of this chapter to recognize that many teachers have a very low level of tolerance, and for some zero tolerance, for accepting language diversity in their classrooms. By adapting the term "zero tolerance" to identify teacher philosophies that hold no consideration for language diversity, we are not suggesting that for speaking nonstandard English, students would be suspended or expelled as if they brandished a gun or a knife in the classroom. Yet according to Stockman, "speakers without speech impairments can be handicapped if their dialect is judged to be inadequate for a particular work or educational setting" (qtd. in Kraemer, Rivers, and Ratusnik 140). Thus, our students' responses also caused us to question whether our preservice courses were helping future teachers to overcome attitudes of low or zero tolerance and if not, why not. Having spent a good deal of our careers combating the proliferation of language myths, these students' comments caused us serious concern.

Our purposes in writing this chapter are threefold: (1) to raise the issue of zero tolerance, which seems to be held by many of the nation's preservice teachers concerning language diversity in the classroom, and to ask what can be done to overcome these attitudes; (2) to report the findings of a recent Internet study of the incorporation of language diversity issues in selected teacher education programs; and (3) to look at a course that not only examines issues of language diversity but also attempts to impact teachers' attitudes concerning language diversity.

Internet Survey of Teacher Education Programs

Ideally, we would have liked to have conducted personal interviews with various department chairs, instructors, and students to determine what is covered in teacher education courses. We acknowledge that oftentimes a segment of a course or lesson may be devoted to language variations, though such topics may not appear in the course description. Still, with access to more than thirteen hundred English departments at our fingertips, we were able to conduct an Internet survey to ascertain the requirements and course descriptions of teacher education programs relative to language diversity. On-line catalogs and/or web pages from a random sample of college or university teacher education programs were examined. A total of twenty-five teacher education programs were analyzed. The web addresses that were used came from New York University professor David L. Hoover's web page that provides links to more than thirteen hundred worldwide public and private college and university English departments. The results revealed that few colleges or universities offer a required course in language diversity for students preparing to become teachers in our nation's schools. In the few programs that did require a course dealing with language diversity, the course generally conceptualized language variation as "dialect differences," incorporating the topic in a broader, comprehensive course such as Introduction to English, History of the English Language, or Introduction to Linguistics. For example, at Adrian College, a small private liberal arts school, English Education students are required to take a course called English Language. In this course, students study "the form, structure, and history of English. Topics may include grammar, syntax, language acquisition, sound and structure changes, the influence of migration and the political implications of language." At Buffalo State College, students majoring in English Education are required to enroll in a course called Foundations of Language, which explores "the significance of regional and social dialects" in addition to other topics.

While our random Internet survey indicated that most American preservice teachers receive little information about language diversity, there are a few innovative programs that provide opportunities for significant studies in language diversity. For example, at California State University–Los Angeles, English Education majors are required to take a course entitled English Language in America, which introduces students to linguistic theory, phonology, and English syntax and discussions on the "levels and functional varieties of usage." Additional electives there provide further opportunities to study language variations, for example, Language and Culture allows students to explore "the nature, origin, and evolution of language" and "studies illustrating variations in the relation of habitual thought and behavior to language." Eastern Michigan University offers School of Education courses in language study, including English Words, African American Language, and Language and Culture. Although it is unlikely that preservice teachers will take all of these electives, exposure to language issues in any one of these courses can enhance their understanding of language variation in their classrooms. For example, the Language and Culture course provides a "survey of the variety of languages and language groups of the world. Topics covered include: origins of human language, language relationships, the ways language changes and why, unusual writing systems, and linguistic exotica."

Our investigation revealed that, even though some students in teacher education programs are offered opportunities to take elective courses that include in-depth discussions on issues of language diversity (such as African American English and History of the English Language), most of the preservice teachers who graduate from institutions that offer such courses never end up taking these courses. That is because the student population in these courses is comprised primarily of currently practicing K–12 classroom teachers who return to the university to upgrade their credentials, linguistics and composition instructors from nearby community colleges, and students majoring in communication disorders who come to the School of Education to take cognate courses. Currently practicing teachers who take these courses praise them for providing eye-opening perspectives and tools for improving their teaching. Teachers who reported taking general language survey courses like Introduction to the English Language continued to express attitudes of zero tolerance toward language diversity in their classrooms. Students who indicated that they had taken courses like African American Dialects and American Dialects generally reflected attitudes that are more tolerant toward the use of language variation in their classrooms.

In a similar vein, although courses like Teaching English as a Second Language and Historical Studies in the English Language have been offered to preservice teachers at some institutions, few preservice teachers actually take these courses unless they are required in their teacher education program. These courses are predominately populated by returning teachers who are seeking further endorsement in additional areas of teaching. All of these courses have been deemed valuable for teachers enrolled in teacher education programs. Further, researchers, scholars, and language educators have contended for the past thirty years that courses offering informed perspectives on language diversity in the classroom should be made an integral part of all teacher preparation programs. Yet almost no preservice teachers take such courses, mainly because there is little space left for them to take additional electives in a curriculum sequence loaded with required courses in their areas of disciplinary concentration.

Our position, then, with regard to preparing future teachers for linguistically diverse classrooms—and, indeed, for a linguistically diverse world—is that at least one course dealing with language variation, bilingualism, and global linguistic diversity should be required of all students in teacher education programs. However, the question remains: If preservice teachers are required to take courses that seriously consider issues of language variation, can these educational experiences help them overcome attitudes of zero tolerance for language diversity in their classrooms? The example that follows is one of many cases that demonstrate that such experiences can indeed make a difference in future teachers' language attitudes.

An Approach to Issues of Language Diversity

This section of the chapter looks at the efforts of one teacher educator, Ball, to expose students to issues of language diversity in a course called The Centralities of Literacies in Teaching and Learning. This is a required course, taken early in the sequence of courses by all preservice teachers in a West Coast teacher education program. The course requires future teachers to explore the close relationship between issues of language and literacy and the social, cultural, and political implications of teachers' understandings of the language and literacy variations that students bring to the classroom. Building on previous research that provides teachers with the knowledge base and strategies for teaching students who speak nonprestige varieties of English, the course is designed to give preservice teachers opportunities to consider the role and function of language and literacies in their lives and in the lives of others and to consider how language and literacies could be used to teach diverse students more effectively.

Before coming into this course, many of the preservice teachers had very limited views about language varieties and literacy practices that were appropriate for use in the classroom. Many of them had also given very little thought to teaching students who were culturally different from them or who had language and literacy histories different from their own. The course introduces preservice teachers to a range of theoretical frameworks that undergird effective teaching of diverse students and provides a safe environment wherein they can question preconceived notions about language variation and literacy. Theoretical texts in the course include excerpts from Richard-Amato and Snow's *The Multicultural Classroom*, which draws attention to cultural considerations when working with "language minority students"; the work of McElroy-Johnson, which cautions teachers about the difficulty of assisting students in developing a voice if they have not yet developed a voice of their own; and the work of Giroux, which challenges teachers to become "transformative intellectuals . . . in order to develop alternative teaching practices . . . capable of shattering the logic of domination both within and outside of schools" (167). These works serve to ignite thoughtful discussions in the course. According to one student,

> although it was difficult at first, once we got over the hump of feeling inadequate about speaking up, the students in our small group discussions were challenged there in ways that reading and writing cannot challenge you. Sometimes we were paired up with the person next to us and discussed passages, issues or situations. On the whole, these exercises were positive learning experiences.

In addition to close readings and discussions of theoretical and practical materials, these preservice teachers were required to engage in classroom tutoring experiences with Latino, African American, Asian, and European American students who were enrolled in an extended educational program. They were also required to implement language and literacy teaching strategies with their students on a daily basis and to complete an adolescent case study that helped them focus on the language and literacy patterns that their students used as well as the literacy approaches that foster student success in the classroom. They also wrote reflective essays and freewriting responses to prompts designed to challenge their thinking. For example, one prompt reminded teachers that critical literacy requires not just that teachers accept students' experiences but also that they help students of diverse backgrounds understand their own experiences, as well as the experiences of others, in terms of the dynamics of the larger society. Another prompt asked teachers to recall their reading of Au, McElroy-Johnson, and Giroux and then to respond to this question: What are your feelings about/ reflections on implementing these types of literacy strategies in your classroom? Another prompt asked these future teachers to take a few moments to imagine the following scenario: You walk into your class on the first day of school. As you look around the room, you notice that the students in your class this year seem to represent an unusually wide range of cultural and linguistic groups—wider than you generally have in your class. In what ways will this change or impact your planning and/or teaching of this class (if at all)?

By the end of the course, these preservice teachers had broadened their perspectives on what it meant for a person to be literate and made them think about ways they could build on students' home language and literacy patterns to more effectively teach students from diverse backgrounds. Indicators of these teachers' broadened perspectives were the serious discussions that took place during class sessions, the broader definitions of literacy they wrote about in their journals, and their plans for using a range of language and literacy activities in their future classrooms. From our analysis of their oral and written discourse, it was clear that these teachers' attitudes about language diversity were changing over time— regardless of whether they came from a European American, Asian American, Latino, or African American background. Illustrative statements that were spoken or written by different preservice teachers at the end of the course included the following:

I've learned to appreciate differences.

[Now I realize that] all students have voices that they manifest in different ways and it is our job as teachers to bring out and help them to realize those voices.

Something that I never appreciated before coming here to this program and to this class was the value of diversity. Talking about the different things that have come up in this class has helped me appreciate the real value of having people from different cultures come together from different places. . . . This class has bridged the gap between theory and practice.

I've never been good at talking in front of people . . . but I read somewhere that kids who can't communicate very well may have higher rates of violence. . . . Well, I think that may be true in some cases because for me in high school I couldn't speak orally very well and things were really building up. But then a teacher realized that I could write well and that was like a release valve for me. . . . Now I realize that all of us teachers have the ability to turn that release valve for our students.

Relative to overcoming attitudes of intolerance in their future classrooms, some preservice teachers said:

The lecture really validated and gave voice to "under-valued" alternative literacies. I realized that it is very important that we all recognize that there are a lot of literacies our students will be utilizing that are not necessarily appreciated in mainstream academic "high culture."

This class has helped me . . . to learn the importance of helping students to feel safe in our classrooms. . . . The challenge that I want to figure out is how to reach all of the kids and know their needs and to meet those needs and how to somehow make it personal, even in the large classroom environment.

Similar opinions were echoed by other preservice teachers as they reflected on the readings they encountered in the course:

The Giroux chapter is asking new teachers to think critically about what we read, write, say and hear . . . to determine its validity for our world of teaching and the worlds of our students. The readings in this class really helped to broaden my perspectives about the uses of language and literacies in our classrooms.

Our readings encouraged us to find our own voices. We

need to recognize and value our own individual strengths
as well as the individual and unique strengths of our students. Students need to be allowed and encouraged to think
and express their ideas in whatever ways that help them
the most. The cookie-cutter lesson plans often handed down
by administrators and governing bodies often only address
one type of learning and literacy. Teachers need to be able
to recognize what they are doing and to meet the individual needs of the students.

In the final analysis, these preservice teachers came to view issues of language and literacy as issues of power and privilege, and
they gained a broadened perspective of their own role in maintain-
ing or dismantling these powers and privileges.

I thought that literacy was only about teaching reading and
writing. But now I see that it's more than that. Literacy is
privilege and it's also about power and voice. It's the way
that we perceive our students as literate individuals and
their voices and how important their voice is.

It came together for me as an understanding of how important a non-threatening class is in order to give these kids
the power and voice they need to have, and that is a very
valid thing in any content area in order to empower students.

My view of literacy has changed. I came in here thinking
that literacy was just reading and writing . . . but now I see
that literacy is access to privilege. I am here to access privilege for my students, and I will teach them to do the same.
. . . I think that literacy is like a color. Like the color blue,
it can take on so many different forms until we can never
really pigeonhole it easily. We know that blue has so many
unique qualities. . . . Well, now I think of discourses as the
different colors that bleed into each other, and I think of

literacy as the brightness of those colors. . . . So, you see, I will take from this class a shift in attitude.

I've learned that teachers have a social responsibility in this world. Our kids come to us with a lot of stuff, but we as teachers have the power to be able to recognize that. We have the power to read into what's going on and to see their literacies and their power and to see that they do have a lot of literacies. There's a lot of ways kids can be literate, and we have to expand that literacy to let them express themselves and see their power. . . . That's our job.

We've been talking a lot about privilege. We've read a lot of articles about what all these other teachers are doing. But we are privileged to be here and to learn so much, and it's our responsibility to share what we are learning with others.

We began this chapter by sharing the voices of preservice teachers who reflect an attitude of zero tolerance about the use of language variation in their future classrooms and raised the question of why these attitudes persist. We went on to share findings from an investigation of the varying amounts of emphasis on language variation in a sample of teacher education programs. We found that enrollment of preservice teachers in courses on language variation is typically low because the curriculum sequence for preservice teachers is loaded with other required courses. We concluded that at least one course dealing with language diversity should be required of all teachers. Finally, we found that when preservice teachers do enroll in well-designed courses that address issues of language and literacy diversity in substantial ways, these future teachers make significant positive changes in their language attitudes.

We here call for further work that will help us develop future teachers who have a broadened understanding of and respect for language variation, who can overcome zero tolerance, and who will even welcome language diversity in their classrooms. We seek to develop future teachers who will grow to become agents of change within current reform efforts to improve our nation's schools.

Works Cited

Au, Kathryn H. *Literacy Instruction in Multicultural Settings*. New York: Harcourt, 1993. 20–34.

Giroux, Henry A. *Teachers as Intellectuals: Toward a Critical Pedagogy of Learning*. New York: Bergin, 1988.

Hoover, David L. *English Department Home Pages Worldwide*. 30 June 2002 <http://www.nyu.edu/gsas/dept/english/links/engdpts.html>.

Kraemer, Robert, Kenyatta O. Rivers, and David L. Ratusnik. "Sociolinguistic Perceptions of African American English." *Negro Educational Review* 51 (2000): 139–48.

McElroy-Johnson, B. "Teaching and Practice: Giving Voice to the Voiceless." *Harvard Educational Review* 63 (1993): 85–104.

Richard-Amato, Patricia A., and Marguerite A. Snow, eds. *The Multicultural Classroom: Readings for Content-Area Teachers*. New York: Addison, 1992.

5 / Practical Pedagogy for Composition
Kim Brian Lovejoy

> If we lived in a democratic state our language would have to
> hurtle, fly, curse, and sing, in all the common American names,
> all the undeniable and unrepresentative and participating
> voices of everybody here.
>
> —June Jordan, *On Call*

The issue of linguistic diversity in the classroom has been a part of
the profession of teaching English for almost forty years, and cer-
tainly it will continue to be a subject of much discussion well into
the current millennium. Of course, such diversity in our language
has always existed, as people use language differently depending on
their regional, social, or cultural affiliation. In fact, variations in our
language, as Sledd points out, "mark differences among people and
their multifarious purposes. Variation in English remains, and has
indeed increased, despite centuries of effort to stamp it out. Its lon-
gevity results from its utility" (317). In the 1960s and 1970s, when
open admissions and desegregation of schools changed the composition of classrooms, teachers came face to face with differences in
their students' language and began to question how to reconcile
such differences with curricular goals. Because of a number of dedicated, forward-thinking, and socially minded teachers who knew
that change would be inevitable if we were to continue to teach and
affect the lives of all our students, we have today the CCCC "National Language Policy" (see Smitherman in this volume) and a
body of research on which to base much needed new developments
in pedagogy—in the ways we deal with language differences and
use those differences to move our students forward to an awareness
of language and an appreciation of their own knowledge and vast
potential as language users.

Despite Smitherman's optimism in recounting the impact of the

CCCC on language rights in the last fifty years ("CCCC's Role" 372), we have not progressed far enough in our pedagogy to address the needs of diverse students. We continue to witness large numbers of students who are not succeeding in our schools and universities. While, on the one hand, Lindemann, in *A Rhetoric for Writing Teachers*, asserts that "we cannot ignore the significant contributions linguists have made in studying how people learn and use English" (62), on the other hand, Lisle and Mano report that "a glance at current rhetorics, which offer a measure of what goes on in most classrooms, suggests that while the profession celebrates heteroglossia and difference, most rhetoric instruction remains monologic and ethnocentric" (12). Our attempts to integrate our students' language differences into our pedagogy and teaching practices, while sporadic, are teeming with possibilities. It is time to close the gap between what we say and what we do in today's classrooms. Otherwise, Jordan's claim that our language is not democratic but rather "the language of the powerful that perpetuates that power through the censorship of dissenting views" (30) becomes our reality. As teachers of English, often the pedagogical leaders in schools and colleges, we need to reexamine our teaching practices and lead other faculty toward an understanding of how to transform existing pedagogy to meet the needs of all students. For unless we can demonstrate to students the value of language differences, we will not have succeeded in communicating to them how such differences contribute to the rich and powerful nuances of our common language—differences that truly reflect our rich cultural heritage.

First, though, I want us to think about what we communicate to students about language use through our teaching and our curricula, and I want to suggest the need for teachers to explore ways we can give students a more informed understanding of language, especially in classrooms designed to teach students academic writing, which, of course, means Edited American English (EAE). My own attempt to integrate language varieties into the teaching of writing has not radically transformed the introductory composition curriculum at my institution, about which I will say more later. Nonetheless, I have begun to implement ways to give students a broader view of language while also preparing them for writing at the college level. My use of linguistic diversity as a resource in teaching writing represents one approach that I hope readers find helpful, and if it leads teachers to rethink their curriculum or to consider other possibilities for classroom practice, I will have achieved my goal. I should say at the start that when I refer to language varieties, I am speaking of varieties of English, whether they be geographical, social, ethnic, or varieties that typify a particular genre such as sports or advertising or rap lyrics.

In a discussion of different varieties of English that I moderated recently in a sophomore-level writing class, one student asked why we should value varieties of English other than EAE. After all, she reasoned, we are in school to be educated, and part of that education is learning how to use language effectively. Those who do not use EAE are just uneducated; they haven't learned the rules. If we come to school to learn to speak using Standard American English and write using EAE, she continued, why should we pretend that it really doesn't matter which variety we use as long as we can understand each other? Everyone knows that standard English is the language that counts.

Suppose, I replied, I receive a phone call from a friend who wants me to play racquetball. I answer the phone; the caller says, "Is Kim there?" And I respond, "This is him. What's up?" Have I misspoken? Have I used language ineffectively? Incorrectly? Invariably, students will say that the correct response is "This is he," and usually someone will even produce the rule: the nominative form of the pronoun, not the objective form, follows a linking verb. But when I protest and say that language should fit the situation—in this case, an informal phone conversation—they look at me and smile as though I'm doing something devious and at the same time liberating. Their conception of language—their teaching or instruction about language—seems too narrowly defined and restrictive to allow them to say it's okay. Yet, as native speakers of English, they unconsciously shift styles in their spoken language every day as they move in and out of different situations of language use. Is writing any different, in this respect?

That prescriptive attitude about written language seems to characterize the thinking of many college students. Somehow, in all the years of taking English and language arts courses in their careers as students, they have come away from their classroom experience with the notion that there is really only one *right* way to use written language—and that's to use EAE. If they've struggled with EAE in the schools, they have little confidence in their abilities to use written language, and some don't even want to try for fear of failure.

In the early 1970s, when teachers expressed concerns about what to do when confronted with "the language habits of students who come from a wide variety of social, economic, and cultural backgrounds" (*Students' Right* 1), the CCCC adopted a resolution (as did NCTE, albeit a significantly weaker version, in 1974) called "Students' Right to Their Own Language." This resolution brought to the forefront the issue of dialects in the classroom and positioned the standard dialect—the language of the schools—in the context of other dialects. It challenged teachers to rethink what they do in the classroom and how they use and respond to students' language. Many teachers interpreted the resolution to mean that they should let their students speak and write any way they want.[1] Many wondered what they were supposed to do, if not teach EAE. Teachers generally understood the need to respect the dialect varieties of their students, but they weren't certain how this policy would affect classroom practice. Consequently, it didn't—the policy failed.

However, the "Students' Right" policy was never intended to diminish the importance of EAE; rather, it was a call for teachers to teach EAE within the context of other Englishes. Smitherman, one of the authors of "Students' Right to Their Own Language," writes that the teaching of EAE "has never been an issue, if and when it has been promoted as an integral part of a policy which includes recognition, use, and acceptance of the native tongue" ("Toward" 31). The recent survey of college and secondary teachers of English, described in Richardson's chapter in this volume, found that English teachers are not prepared to cope with the diverse students in their classrooms. A significant number of teachers not only had not received the kind of training they believed was necessary but also were unaware of the published positions of their professional organizations about the legitimacy and richness of language diversity (*Language*). Ball and Lardner, writing about the historic Ann Arbor Black English court case and the continued poor performance of African American students in urban schools, stated in a recent article that

> research on language attitudes consistently indicates that teachers believe African American English speaking children are "nonverbal" and possess limited vocabularies. Speakers of African American English are often perceived to be slow learners or uneducable; their speech is often considered to be unsystematic and in need of constant correction and improvement. (472)

Resistance to language that does not conform to EAE or to "correct" English usage—the language of the schools—can be felt in classrooms at every educational level. It may be a resistance to Black Vernacular English, to Chicano English, to rural and working-class dialects, or to any other variety of nonmainstream English. Clearly, we want all students to develop a proficiency in EAE in order to gain access to the dominant culture, but if it is the only form of writing required of students, we not only exclude our students' home languages—their natural language abilities—but also distort the power and capacity of language to communicate in the written mode. As Elbow has articulated, academic discourse as it is commonly taught should not ignore "the everyday or common or popular in language" ("Reflections" 145). Given the growing diversity of our students and the social implications of language prejudice (the relatively recent attacks on Ebonics in the Oakland School District is a prime example), it seems reasonable to ask what we are doing in the writing and language arts classroom to promote an understanding of language varieties and their uses. And learning to appreciate such diversity is predicated on one's informed attitudes about language uses. As language educators, it is our responsibility to teach not only the language of power but also the multiplicity of ways we use language to communicate every day.

The problems that teachers experienced in the classroom in the early 1970s are all the more apparent today. Our world is becoming increasingly more diverse, multilingual, and multicultural. It is happening in central states like Indiana at a slower pace than in other parts of the country, but it is happening nevertheless. Increasing numbers of minorities and nontraditional students are entering the mainstream in today's classrooms, and our students will need to be prepared to interact with, work with, and respect people from many different walks of life. Writing about American bilingual students, Valdés asserts that

> composition specialists must begin to see the "new" student population not as a special group destined to disappear quickly into the mainstream but as a population that will significantly change the character of the entire student community in this country. (128)

Businesses have already begun to take steps to educate their workers about intercultural communication and language issues. Our National Language Policy, adopted by CCCC in 1988 and subsequently by NCTE, is a renewed challenge to English teachers to embrace the differences that characterize our national culture and to begin to transform our pedagogy to meet the needs of diverse learners.

The Challenge of Diversity

I teach in an English department with a writing program that offers multiple sections of first-year writing courses for students throughout the university. All students, for example, take Elementary Composition I, a process-oriented course that uses portfolios as a means of instruction and assessment. We are continually assessing the effectiveness of our writing courses and revising to better meet the needs of our students and the expectations of faculty in the university. In recent years, however, the move has been to infuse more rigor into the curriculum, meaning more of the traditional academic, research-based writing, in large part due to pressure from faculty in other disciplines. In such a climate, it is challenging to have to move in the direction of uniformity, on the one hand, while also trying to create an environment that recognizes and values diversity, on the other. Teachers at the elementary and secondary levels have their own special challenges, such as standardized testing and overcrowded classrooms, but my point here is to suggest that even given the obstacles we face, we must ensure there is always space in the curriculum to invite and explore language as it is used by our students and in the world around us. We should also remember that when we face controversies in the curriculum, it is at these critical junctures that faculty can come together to discuss important issues and to educate one another about language attitudes and language learning.

To meet the challenge of diversity, English teachers must begin to fill the gaps in knowledge created by teacher preparation programs that emphasize literary study with little, if any, attention given to the teaching of writing in a diverse culture. Several excellent books and articles on language and diversity can provide teachers with a knowledge base to respond to their students' questions and to develop appropriate curricula and learning activities. Labov's *Study of Nonstandard English* is an important early work that describes important sociolinguistic principles necessary for an understanding of nonstandard dialects; it also includes discussion of specific educational problems in reading, writing, and speaking. Kutz's *Language and Literacy: Studying Discourse in Communities and Classrooms* provides a useful introduction to the study of language as it is used by speakers and writers in a variety of contexts and demonstrates how one's native language abilities form the basis for new learning and for the acquisition of new discourses in schools and universities. Severino, Guerra, and Butler's *Writing in Multicultural Settings,* a collection of essays, offers theoretical and practical insights on the teaching of writing in multicultural college classrooms, with particular attention to the issues and cultural tensions that arise. Other equally important and insightful readings can be found in the annotated bibliography in this volume. But a word of caution here: If we have learned anything from our failed attempts as practitioners to recognize and legitimize linguistic diversity, it would be that a cognitive understanding and appreciation of language differences is not sufficient. Once we acquire a knowledge base, we must take the difficult step of translating that knowledge into meaningful classroom practices that can shape our students' view of language and their experiences as writers. As the contributors to Schroeder, Fox, and Bizzell's *Alt Dis* demonstrate, teachers are beginning to explore and value new ways of writing that enable students to produce intellectual work using their own varieties of language while drawing, as needed, on the forms and features of traditional academic writing. As more teachers develop their pedagogies to accommodate diverse students and their linguistic differences, we will begin to see the kind of programmatic changes in writing programs that can have an impact on large numbers of students and create an environment for teachers to share best practices and to talk, reflectively and productively, about issues of linguistic diversity in the classroom.

Meeting the challenge of diversity means that teachers will need to rethink their pedagogy and become reflective practitioners, learning to take risks in the classroom in responsible, productive ways. Cope and Kalantzis, in the recent *Multiliteracies,* write about an ambitious international multiliteracy project that responds to our linguistic and cultural differences and to the multimodal ways (linguistic, visual, audio, gestural, and so on) in which meanings are communicated in a technologically advanced society.[2] These changes, they argue, will "transform both the substance and pedagogy of literacy teaching," for "the old pedagogies of a formal, standard, written national language" are no longer adequate (6). To prepare teachers for a new literacy pedagogy, they propose a pedagogical model that builds on what teachers already do in their classrooms. The model is useful because it supplements existing teaching practices and suggests ideas and strategies for teachers to incorporate into their teaching. The model focuses on four aspects of literacy instruction: situated practice (student-centered learning), overt instruction (teacher-centered instruction), critical framing (critical literacy), and transformed practice (applied learning, theory into practice). These four different aspects of teaching characterize "the main traditions in literacy teaching, problematic as each of these may be in their more doctrinaire and isolated forms" (Kalantzis and Cope 240). Kalantzis and Cope argue that all four are necessary to good teaching, and they are best used together in combinations that are fluid and nonlinear: "For when all four aspects are put together in various combinations each is, at least, softened and, at best, enhanced and transformed by the others" (240). I suggest this model as a good starting point because it offers teachers a positive way to think about their teaching and strategies to further enhance their students' learning. The exercises and challenges I describe in the next section illustrate a range of learning activities, from overt instruction to transformed practice, that characterize literacy pedagogy.

Classroom Practices

I have begun to integrate classroom activities and assignments that give students exposure to different varieties of English and that create opportunities for students to explore their language. One way to address language differences is first to create an environment in which students feel comfortable sharing their ideas and observations about language. If teachers want to know what their students think about *English*, for example, they need only invite them to write about it. What does *English* mean to you? What comes to mind—what pops into your head—when you think about *English?* Journal writing at the beginning of class is a productive way to get students thinking about topics for discussion. Teachers may be surprised, even startled, by some student perceptions and attitudes about English, but the exercise is a good opener and an effective way to begin a discussion of language and how it works.

I start early in the course by talking about how we acquire

language, how speech and writing differ, what we mean by *grammar,* what academic writing entails (for example, the ability to summarize, synthesize, integrate and document other voices, support and argue claims), and what other language varieties exist that we don't often hear about in schools and universities. In talking about grammar, a source of anxiety for many students, I ask them to complete short exercises that draw on their knowledge of grammar. One exercise, for example, asks them to reconstruct a scrambled list of words (four, the, American, women, beautiful) into an English noun phrase and then to formulate the rules that enabled them to arrange the words into a sensible phrase. McPherson uses a similar exercise: She gives students a list of words in alphabetical order (a, badly, cafeteria, needs, new, school, this, very) and then asks students to construct a meaningful sentence (90). Because of their intuitive knowledge of grammar, students have no difficulty completing the exercises. They struggle, of course, with formulating the rules governing their choices but only because they are native speakers.

When we talk about the language varieties that students don't often hear about in the schools, one of the simplest and most informative graphic illustrations I like to use is from a work on language diversity by Moss and Walters. It illustrates what we focus on in the schools and what often gets left out (see fig. 5.1).

This simple diagram illustrates the narrow, limited scope of our teaching about language in the classroom and the expansive territory left virtually unexplored. This is the territory I explore with my students. After introducing some examples of nonmainstream varieties (for example, rap lyrics, advertisements, excerpts from fiction), I invite students to bring in samples of writing or kinds of language that would fall in the "everything else" space in the diagram. These samples of writing provide the subject matter for class discussions of language uses, for analyses of written discourse, and for class work on the differences between EAE and other varieties.

Along these same lines, I also emphasize, throughout the semester, the importance of understanding the writing/speaking situation (reader/listener, writer/speaker, subject, purpose, focus, and

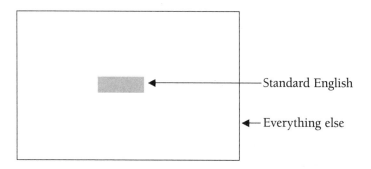

Fig. 5.1. The view of language promulgated by schools. From Moss and Walters 144, © 1993 by the Board of Trustees, Southern Illinois University, reprinted by permission of the publisher.

event) and learning to make rhetorical and linguistic choices that fit the context in which language is being used. By emphasizing the context or situation for writing, I try to get students to see that judgments about a language variety outside of a context are groundless and are often, if not always, attacks on the speaker or user of the language rather than the language itself.

One goal of the course is for students to be able to define a writing situation and to produce a piece of writing that reflects their ability to make good choices. Toward this end, we analyze samples of writing, including the students' own, that reflect different purposes and audiences. One assignment, for example, asks students to read Langston Hughes's "Mother to Son," a short poem in which the speaker, a mother addressing her son, uses a nonmainstream variety.

> Well, son, I'll tell you:
> Life for me ain't been no crystal stair.
> It's had tacks in it
> And splinters,
> And boards torn up,
> And places with no carpet on the floor—
> Bare.

But all the time
I'se been a-climbin' on,
And reachin' landin's
And turnin' corners,
And sometimes goin' in the dark
Where there ain't been no light.
So boy, don't you turn back.
Don't you set down on the steps
'Cause you finds it's kinder hard.
Don't you fall now—
For I'se still goin', honey,
I'se still climbin',
And life for me ain't been no crystal stair.

After identifying some of the nonmainstream features of the poem, we discuss the meanings of the poem, the effectiveness and significance of the extended metaphor, and the appropriateness of the language. How does the language of the poem contribute to the writer's purpose? How would the poem sound if it were written in EAE? This exercise also gives teachers an opportunity to talk about language appropriateness, as opposed to correctness, as a criterion for evaluating effectiveness in a piece of writing. Students may then work on writing their own poem or a short prose piece that uses a nonmainstream language variety to communicate an idea or emotion.

Alternatively, students may choose to create a dialogue like the one written by a student who visited a Vermont sugar-on-snow festival during the maple season. Here, for example, she captures a language variety as she shares a conversation she had with a farmer about the maple industry:

> *Student:* How many trees d'ya tap?
> *Farmer:* All them trees on the far side [pointing to the mountain] we'll tap for syrup come winter.
> *Student:* And how long will it take ya to collect it all?
> *Farmer:* Oh, not long a t'all. Years ago we hitched the horses to sleds, but them days are long gone. Now we pull 'em

with skidoos and it don't take no time. Fill that vat over yonder [pointing to a large container for boiling the sap] in half a day. Before it was weeks.

Student: And then you boil it?

Farmer: Yep, only an ounce of syrup fer a gallon of sap. That's a lot of work 'cause most of it you jes' watch go up in vapor.

Student: That hardly seems worth the effort.

Farmer: You say that if you don't like the syrup, but most people do. It ain't called liquid gold fer nothin'.

The value of this exercise is that it teaches students that language is multifaceted and, in the written mode, capable of communicating meaning in various forms and styles.

Students who find it easier to conform to EAE should have opportunities to stretch and to use other language varieties in their writing. Once students generate these pieces of writing, they can then write expository or multigenre papers on the same subject but for a different situation, one that perhaps requires the writer's attention to EAE. But by sensitizing students to language varieties, the exercises also open the way for students to use their own language in the paper assignments. One of the formal paper assignments, for example, asks students to reflect on some of the stories told by members of their family—stories told by a mother or father, an older sibling, or a grandparent; stories about other family members in their youth or about achievements or disappointments; humorous stories or sad ones. Students choose a story to tell in their papers and then analyze the story's significance or the message it conveys. What I have found is that students are more likely to experiment and take risks in their writing—or just relax and use their natural language—if they are not concentrating so much on a particular style of writing that they associate with EAE.

When we begin to introduce various texts from outside the classroom, or real-world writing, we can talk about the rhetorical and linguistic choices writers make. An advertisement for Dodge Intrepid that appeared in *Time* magazine, for example, takes the last syllable in *technology* and creates the utterance *Gee,* then uses it in the caption of the ad—"It puts the 'Gee' in Technology" (see fig. 5.2).

A cursory examination of the text and graphical illustrations reveal the advertisement's focus on technological innovations. Putting students in groups to collaborate on a text analysis of the ad—for example, analyzing lexical chains—is one way to help students understand how a writer establishes and maintains focus. It is also an opportunity to examine features of a language variety—for example, the use of fragments, which are often treated pejoratively in the writing classroom.

Notice that the text of the ad begins and ends with sentence fragments (often considered nonmainstream in school writing but commonly used in ads) and that the two complete sentences are tucked inconspicuously in the middle. Why do these complete sentences occur in the middle of the text? Why do the fragments occur where they do? Are they used effectively? How would the ad read if all the sentences were complete? Students might then experiment with language by writing a piece composed largely of sentence fragments. In the following example, one student chose to write about a strong emotion—anger:

> Anger. It just sits there inside. Building and building. Laughing at you each time you try to fight it. Feeding on your suffering. Growing bigger. It just stays there in your stomach. In your heart. Body. Soul. Holding all this inside doesn't pay off. It gets worse. Like an explosive about to detonate. I see no way to get beyond it. Trapped within the circle. Thinking I'm surfacing. Really going nowhere. Anger isn't pleasant. But even though this is all true, I go back. Get consumed. There's no getting rid of it.

This may seem like a relatively easy exercise, and some teachers may even argue that it is not the kind of writing we should be encouraging students to do. But to do it effectively, students need to pay attention to the progression of their ideas and to the rhythm and flow of their sentences or non-sentences. Some students approach the

		than some city apartments? Gee. These are merely a few examples of the technological artistry behind Dodge Intrepid ES Although born in the virtual world of ones and zeroes, Dodge Intrepid remains an automobile best appreciated in the	real world. On real curves. Where you can experience the pulse-quickening sensations of sudden acceleration, brisk braking, and athletic cornering. Dodge Intrepid. A technical masterpiece. And a simple joy.
An automatic transmission that lets you decide when to shift? Gee. An available aluminum 225 horsepower, 3.2 liter V-6, designed and proven in cyberspace? Gee. A	sleek cab-forward sedan that feels roomier		
	It puts the "Gee" in technology.		

Fig. 5.2. Advertisement for Dodge Intrepid. From *Time* 24 Jan. 2000: 24–25.

exercise by writing complete sentences and then breaking them up to create fragments, and the result is artificial and ineffective. Another activity is to have students write their own ad copy for products they know well, and then write reflectively about their linguistic and rhetorical choices. For a more formal piece of writing, students can analyze the content and style of an ad and evaluate the writer's choices in the context in which the ad appears.

Students need opportunities to examine language in various forms and styles—to explore the uses of spoken language at home and in school and the uses of written language in poetry and plays, in advertising and sports writing, in personal letters and in fiction, in notes to friends and in e-mail messages, and in academic settings or forums. In other words, I aim to help students learn the forms and the conventions of EAE, but not by excluding other varieties of English.

In a recent article entitled "Inviting the Mother Tongue: Beyond

'Mistakes,' 'Bad English,' and 'Wrong Language,'" Elbow writes about the "conflicting goals or obligations" that he believes most teachers of college writing have experienced. It is the conflict between getting students to learn EAE so that they can succeed in their college classes and in the work world and, on the other hand, respecting students' linguistic differences by allowing them to use their own dialect or mother tongue. He offers a "pragmatic" proposal for doing both in the writing classroom. His goal is to create a "safe place" for nonmainstream language (361).

What he proposes is allowing students to use their own mother tongue as they work on their essays in draft form. In this way, Elbow says, the teacher can focus on matters of content such as focus, development, and organization. But when the writer nears the final draft, it is the writer's responsibility to see that it conforms to the conventions of EAE. He suggests that students get help with editing if they need it, whether it means going to the Writing Center, meeting with him in conference, or hiring someone to do the editing for them. The important point, in Elbow's view, is that students learn to take responsibility for their writing, and if it means hiring someone to edit their papers, then that is a responsible alternative.

Elbow builds a strong case for allowing students to write in their mother tongue. He creates a path for teachers to follow—for teachers to begin figuring out for themselves what this will mean for their own teaching practices. His long-term goal is "to honor and help preserve multiple dialects of English and to legitimize their use in writing" ("Inviting" 378). But as the following quote illustrates, he is not prepared to accept the mother tongue in the final papers his students produce:

> We can invite students to leave their exercises and low stakes writing in the home dialect—helping send the message that nonmainstream dialects don't need to be "corrected" in SWE [Standard Written English] to be legitimate. And even on major essays, we can invite copy-editing into two final drafts: one into correct SWE and one into the best form of the student's home dialect. (378)

But why must students convert every essay they write to SWE? Not all pieces of writing can or should be transformed into SWE (or, more precisely, Edited American English). If a student writes a personal essay about a family story and elects to use the mother tongue in constructing the piece, and the language suits the writer's purpose, then shouldn't that suffice? One of my students is now in the process of writing a family story in African American Language, and it is rich in detail and emotion. It is a moving story about his family: the father loses his job, the boy goes to school, some of the kids tease him about his father not having work, and he gets into a fight, ends up in the principal's office, and then worries about the "whuppin" he's going to get when he gets home. His younger sister rats on him, and he knows he will have to settle up with his father. The paper builds to that final confrontation:

> "Buster come here," dad called in a tone of voice I had never heard before, and I could feel the pain. Explain to me why you and Marvin were fighting! Tears rolled down my eyes as I begin to explain. The next thing I knew dad said with a smile, are you all right? I heard you got your butt dusted. Boy, you don't know how to take care of yourself? Everything will be fine you don't have to fight everybody that says something mean to you just hold your head high look them straight in the face and walk away. That was the best news I had heard all day. And a bit of good news too because at this point I knew that the butt whuppin I thought I was going to get was not coming. I smiled and asked dad what are we going to do now that we got to move? Son he replied, that's me and your momma concern you just take care of yourself and don't let me hear you fighting any more. I love that man, he was my dad and I was proud of him no matter what. Three weeks later we moved.

While I would want to point out to this student inconsistencies in print-code features, such as the use of quotation marks to signal direct speech and other marks of punctuation, I would not want this writer to lose those features of African American Language. How is this paper different, in its use of language, from the Langston Hughes poem? Wouldn't we rob the piece of its unique qualities, its distinctive tone, if we required the student to write in the style of the academy? There should be an opportunity for students to feature such a piece in a final portfolio.

I want my students to learn to make thoughtful decisions in their writing, decisions that are based on purpose and audience and context. I want them to see how some pieces can be written appropriately in the students' own language while other pieces are more appropriate in EAE. And even within EAE, there is room for variation.[3] That is the direction I am taking in my own introductory writing classes—getting students to fit their writing to the situation for which it is intended and helping them to make careful decisions about their writing on that basis.

Language diversity has been a central issue for as long as composition has existed as a discipline, and in the last forty years the field has undergone major shifts in its beliefs about language and the teaching of writing. The shift to a process-oriented curriculum redefined the traditional roles of teacher and student and established individualized conferences, collaborative learning, self-reflective writing, and portfolio assessment as important teaching and learning tools. Indeed, teachers and researchers have forged dramatic changes in the writing classroom, and the move to recognize and legitimize language varieties is upon us. We cannot fail in our pedagogy to encompass the diversity of our students. How we respond to our students' language is a challenge we all face. And how we encourage and inspire our students to find meaning through language —in all its varieties—is a goal I believe we will achieve.

Notes

The poem "Mother to Son" is from *The Collected Poems of Langston Hughes* by Langston Hughes, copyright © 1994 by the Estate of Langston Hughes. Used by permission of Alfred A. Knopf, a division of Random House, Inc.

1. See, for example, Pixton, Smith.

2. For the sheer joy of reading a multimodal text, see *As the Future Catches You* (New York: Crown Business, 2001), written by Harvard professor of business Juan Enriquez.

3. See, for example, the work of Romano.

Works Cited

Ball, Arnetha, and Ted Lardner. "Dispositions Toward Language: Teacher Constructs and the Ann Arbor Black English Case." *CCC* 48 (1997): 469–85.

CCCC Language Policy Committee. *Language Knowledge and Awareness Survey.* Final Report. Jan. 2000 <http://www.ncte.org/cccc/langsurvey.pdf>.

———. *The National Language Policy.* Urbana, IL: NCTE, 1991 (brochure).

Cope, Bill, and Mary Kalantzis. "Introduction: Multiliteracies: The Beginnings of an Idea." Cope and Kalantzis 3–8.

———, eds. *Multiliteracies: Literacy Learning and the Design of Social Futures.* New York: Routledge, 2000.

Elbow, Peter. "Inviting the Mother Tongue: Beyond 'Mistakes,' 'Bad English,' and 'Wrong Language.'" *Journal of Advanced Composition: A Journal of Composition Theory* 19.3 (1999): 359–99.

———. "Reflections on Academic Discourse: How It Relates to Freshmen and Colleagues." *College English* 53.2 (Feb. 1991): 135–55.

Farr, Marcia, and Harvey Daniels. *Language Diversity and Writing Instruction.* ERIC Clearinghouse on Reading and Communication Skills. Urbana, IL: NCTE, 1986.

Hughes, Langston. "Mother to Son." *The Collected Poems of Langston Hughes.* Ed. Arnold Rampersad and David Roessel. New York: Knopf, 1995.

Jordan, June. *On Call: Political Essays.* Boston: South End, 1985.

Kalantzis, Mary, and Bill Cope. "A Multiliteracies Pedagogy: A Pedagogical Supplement." Cope and Kalantzis 239–48.

Kutz, Eleanor. *Language and Literacy: Studying Discourse in Communities and Classrooms.* Portsmouth, NH: Boynton, 1997.

Labov, William. *The Study of Nonstandard English.* Center for Applied Linguistics, Washington, D.C. 1969. Rev. ed. Urbana, IL: NCTE, 1981.

Lindemann, Erika. *A Rhetoric for Writing Teachers.* 3rd ed. New York: Oxford UP, 1995.

Lisle, Bonnie, and Sandra Mano. "Embracing a Multicultural Rhetoric." *Writing in Multicultural Settings.* Ed. Carol Severino, Juan C. Guerra, and Johnnella E. Butler. New York: MLA, 1997. 12–26.

McPherson, Elisabeth. "Language: Unites or Divides? The Students' Right in Retrospect." *Literacy as a Human Problem.* Ed. James C. Raymond. University: U of Alabama P, 1982. 73–96.

Moss, Beverly J., and Keith Walters. "Rethinking Diversity: Axes of Difference in the Writing Classroom." *Theory and Practice in the Teaching of Writing: Rethinking the Discipline.* Ed. Lee Odell. Carbondale: Southern Illinois UP, 1993. 132–85.

Pixton, William H. "A Contemporary Dilemma: The Question of Standard English." *CCC* 25.4 (Oct. 1974): 247–53.

Romano, Tom. *Writing with Passion: Life Stories, Multiple Genres.* Portsmouth, NH: Boynton, 1995.

Schroeder, Christopher, Helen Fox, and Patricia Bizzell, eds. *Alt Dis: Alternative Discourses and the Academy.* Portsmouth, NH: Boynton, 2002.

Severino, Carol, Juan C. Guerra, and Johnnella E. Butler, eds. *Writing in Multicultural Settings.* New York: MLA, 1997.

Sledd, James H. "Standard English and the Study of Variation: 'It All Be Done for a Purpose.'" *Language Variation in North American English: Research and Teaching.* Ed. Wayne Glowka and Donald M. Lance. New York: MLA, 1993. 275–81.

Smith, Allen N. "No One Has a Right to His Own Language." *CCC* 27 (1976): 155–59.

Smitherman, Geneva. "CCCC's Role in the Struggle for Language Rights." *CCC* 50 (1999): 349–76.

———. "Toward a National Public Policy on Language." *College English* 49.1 (Jan. 1987): 29–36.

Students' Right to Their Own Language. Spec. issue of *CCC* 25 (1974): 1–32.

Valdés, Guadalupe. "Bilingual Minorities and Language Issues in Writing." *Written Communication* 9.1 (Jan. 1992): 85–136.

6 / "Resurfacing Roots"

Developing a Pedagogy of Language Awareness
from Two Views

Gail Y. Okawa

My attitudes have grown since I discovered and resurfaced the
roots behind the closed minded attitudes. . . . As you resurface
the roots of your language attitudes you can begin to change
them.

—Jeanine, student

For many people, even teachers who make language their business,
the roots of language attitudes are buried deep within our personal,
family, and community histories and experience. Until I left my
home in Hawai'i to study and begin my teaching career on the
mainland, for example, I had little appreciation for the regional dialect that I grew up hearing; until I began to study sociolinguistics, I
didn't understand why I felt that way. Yet, in U.S. history, positive
and negative feelings about one's own and other people's ways of
speaking have justified discrimination, segregated school children,
privileged others, and served as a reason for social advancement or
degradation, a point of solidarity or divisiveness, a basis for economic assimilation or exclusion.

These attitudes continue to have frightening consequences today. The CCCC Language Policy Committee study giving rise to
this book has revealed that although many CCCC members are relatively knowledgeable about language issues, a considerable gap in
knowledge and exposure exists among educators at the pre-college
level (CCCC Language Policy Committee, *Language Knowledge and
Awareness Survey*). Significantly and disturbingly, the degree of sociolinguistic awareness and intolerant practice in many cases can be
correlated with race (Okawa and Richardson). As U.S. society becomes increasingly complex, especially in terms of linguistic and

109

cultural diversity, the educational, economic, and ethical stakes are clearly too high for teachers to turn a blind eye to issues of linguistic human rights[1] and linguistic imperialism.[2] After decades of teaching hundreds of college and university students, I find it increasingly imperative to foster the development of a cross-cultural and meta-linguistic awareness in each of my classes—especially among pre-service and in-service teachers regarding their own language and that of others—what one of those students, Jeanine, referred to as "resurfac[ing] the roots" of our language attitudes. This is, after all, a matter of social justice.

Learning Pedagogy by Teaching

Over the last few years, primarily with prospective elementary and secondary school teachers like Jeanine, I have been developing more or less effective ways of approaching Introduction to Language, a rigorous sophomore-level English course required of and designed primarily for these preservice education majors. By teaching it, I am continually learning how challenging subject matter may be trans-lated through teaching into learning. In doing so, I am developing a Pedagogy of Language Awareness for my own teaching, for the consideration of the future teachers in my classes, and, in these pages, for the colleagues who share my concern. Here, I use the term *pedagogy* in the broadest Freirean sense—in terms of what Richard Shaull describes as "a process of reflection which is set in a thoroughly historical context, which is carried out in the midst of a struggle to create a new social order and thus represents a new unity of theory and *praxis*" (12).

In this chapter, I begin by exploring facets of *unawareness* de-scribed by students—but applicable to teachers as well—in order to contextualize the needs that this pedagogy must address. I then suggest a pedagogy of multidimensional reflection that may apply broadly. Finally, to teachers of culturally and linguistically diverse backgrounds, particularly scholars of Color, I propose a further con-sideration and challenge.

Unawareness *Defined*

As native speakers of their own language varieties, students at all levels are developing a working sensitivity to the nuances of meaning and speech as any normal speaker of a language would. However, in reflective essays written at the end of each term, many of my students attempt to characterize the lack of metalinguistic awareness that they felt prior to their study in this course, thereby revealing different facets of unawareness. Some see their un-consciousness in terms of not thinking about language before, of taking it for granted; others like Jeanine are refreshingly candid in describing their "closed mindedness," how judgmental—"too quick to judge" —they have been toward others who don't speak as they do. Some attribute this to being "ethnocentric" or "stupid" or "immature."[3] Theirs is a closed or narrow-mindedness based on ignorance, on literally not knowing, on *not yet* developing a metalinguistic vantage for seeing how language operates in their lives.

This unawareness leaves them susceptible to believing and upholding myths that may be destructive to others, and ultimately themselves, for some students internalize linguistic colonialism as both victims and perpetrators of discrimination. One writer, whose native tongue is African American Language (AAL), referred to feeling "a hidden shame" of her language, "a shame born from a lack of knowledge regarding my history." Others are limited by their own value judgments regarding the speech of others, as some students come to recognize. In the context of my classes and the culture of the region, racial discrimination and internalized racism are often inseparable from intolerant attitudes toward different languages and dialects.[4]

Dimensions of Reflection

As I have written elsewhere, I have learned from my students over the years that "ignorance of language as systematic social behavior with historical roots is one of the greatest co-conspirators of linguistic chauvinism and internalized linguistic imperialism" (Okawa, "From 'Bad Attitudes'" 278). Although Jeanine's metaphor in the opening epigraph may seem somewhat naive to some readers, it is useful here in depicting how unencumbered we are with such language attitudes to begin with, yet how deeply and insidiously they become rooted in the ways we perceive ourselves and others as we grow older. One of the challenges to teachers—all teachers of prospective teachers and of students in secondary and college composition classrooms—is to develop and to help their students develop both the motivation and tools to "resurface the roots" of language use and language attitudes, to develop in them the theoretical and practical understanding of language as social behavior, so that they have the means to make their own informed, humane decisions in life and in the classroom. Self-awareness may be one path to language awareness.

Put another way, this process requires what John Mayher refers to as "uncommonsense"; based on the idea that we are guided most powerfully by notions we hold unconsciously, this process is interpreted by Keith Gilyard as an "empirical questioning of common sense ideas and a commitment to examine our received wisdom at the conscious level" (*Let's Flip the Script* 17). It requires what James Sledd describes as "a still deeper questioning, directed toward deeper social awareness among both teachers and students" ("Grammar for Social Awareness" 37)—a kind of de-construction of unconscious language behavior and language attitudes leading to the re-construction of knowledge and language awareness.

Learning Community and Regional History

When I began to teach Intro to Language upon arrival at my current institution over eight years ago, I had developed my syllabus in a kind of vacuum as an introduction to language in social context.[5] I had designed the course to provide preservice education majors with knowledge of language as a phenomenon that is dynamic, socially constructed, and changing, with an understanding of language acquisition and with experience as language observers and "researchers." We would study how language is influenced by culture, class, geography, and gender, producing its myriad language varieties and controversies, as well as matters of language policy. A generic introduction to language.

But, of course, students are not generic. Although the subject matter could stand on its own as being interesting—one of my first students in this class, now a university instructor, has told me that the course changed her perception of and interest in language—she and other receptive students were counterbalanced and sometimes outnumbered by the resistant and disengaged. In teaching thirteen sections of this course on a ten-week quarter system and six more on semesters, I have learned that becoming familiar with the region and adapting course material to this *particular* linguistic and social context and these *particular* students are essential to transformations in students' perceptions of language and of themselves and others as language users.

As varied as those linguistic and social contexts and students may be throughout the United States, permit me to provide a brief description from my experience as a case in point. I teach at a state university in what some automobile manufacturers have referred to as the "heartland of America." Located in the heart of a small Midwestern city in the Rust Belt, it is largely a commuter campus, and students with few exceptions stop by, pick up their education, and return to the surrounding provincial communities. The university's approximately 12,000 students are predominantly European Americans from the city and surrounding suburban and rural communities, many of them children, grandchildren, and great-grandchildren of the steel mill workers who immigrated to the area from eastern and southern Europe during steel's heyday. Students in my classes have cited such cultural and linguistic heritages as Italian, Slovak, Polish, Greek, Ukrainian, Croatian, Romanian, and Hungarian, in addition to Irish, Scots, English, German, and French, with the occasional student of Color being of African American or Puerto Rican descent.

Between 1977 and 1981, many mills shut down, leaving thousands jobless and leading to the closing of hundreds of businesses. The consequences of these events continue to be felt over two decades later. In analyzing the challenges they encountered while teaching at the same university in the early 1990s, Sherry Linkon and Bill Mullen describe the socioeconomic and political context:

> Economic depression and the strong, steadfastly separate ethnic cultures of Youngstown have contributed to the development of a generally divisive, conservative culture in the region. By far the strongest and most hostile division has developed between whites and blacks. Historically, this may be traced to the role African Americans played as company-imported strikebreakers and competitors in the labor pool as early as the 1930s. More recently, the division reflects de facto segregation caused by white flight. . . . [W]hite students, many of whom attended all-white suburban high schools, often encounter blacks for the first time in the classroom and on campus. (27–28)

In addition to European Americans and African Americans, Latinos, primarily of Puerto Rican backgrounds, have had a presence in the region since the 1940s, while those who identify with various American Indian and Asian American groups are present but nearly invisible. Clearly, this is a potentially volatile environment for discussing cultural and linguistic diversity. Yet understanding these relationships and discussing or framing language experience in the context of such historical and social circumstances can make the students' memories, lives, attitudes, and reflections a central text of the course, providing continually fresh grist for the mill of the innovative and reflective teacher.

Social Histories of U.S. Languages and Dialects: Case Examples

One way of examining a phenomenon as intangible, transparent, and taken for granted as language in tangible terms is to introduce students to the multicultural/multilingual complexity of the continent's population according to different layers of language users over historical time.[6] This approach dispels the myth that "America =

English." Beginning with the myriad American Indian languages, reflecting the diverse cultural and linguistic groups throughout the continent before Contact, students can become familiar with the relationships between people and their languages—how social and political relationships can determine the fate of both.[7] In describing the experience of Native peoples with imperialism, linguistic and otherwise, during and after Contact, I introduce concepts like language maintenance, language shift, language loss, language death,[8] and linguistic human rights. Concepts like these may also be useful to students in their documentation of their personal family language histories (see below). Time permitting, I sometimes use clips from films like *Thunderheart* and *Lakota Woman* to illustrate linguistic and cultural imperialism.

The second layer is composed of languages of the invading powers, the Colonial languages of the "old settlers," principally Spanish, English, French, and German, resulting in the expansion of English as the lingua franca and the subsequent jockeying for power among the speakers of those Colonial tongues in U.S. history.[9] These events provide a useful frame of reference for contemporary language struggles.

African languages like Hausa, Ibo, and Yoruba[10] comprise the third layer and served to add still greater complexity to the multilingual character of U.S. language history, a point driven home by the hour-long documentary "Black on White" in *The Story of English* video series. The film traces the origins of Black English (now African American Language) to West Africa and the slave trade and depicts the influences of AAL on dialects spoken by other Americans, providing a historical framework to give students a context for current language practices. Because the city's schoolchildren are predominantly African American and because education students often must observe, do internships, and/or student teach in the local schools, an extended sociolinguistic study of AAL is critical in helping prospective teachers understand more clearly the intersections among language, culture, and identity.

Perhaps most important for future teachers, we read Keith Gilyard's *Voices of the Self: A Study of Language Competence* so that students can become aware of the complexities of a bidialectal child's language experience. Through Gilyard's autobiographical narrative and sociolinguistic analysis, they can see language acquisition, communicative competence, codeswitching, and language politics, among other things, at play in concrete terms. They see Keith becoming Raymond as he switches codes and identities to survive in his different environments. In this case, my best laid plans seem to have the desired effect, for some students explicitly comment on the insights they have gained through this reading. In an overview of the course one quarter, Lonnie, a Head Start teacher, wrote:

> I really think that it was essential to read Gilyard. It is important to know that language varieties, [such] as Black English, are rule-governed and have structure. Gilyard's book also showed how teachers can affect a student's learning through their acceptance of all aspects of the student.

Speakers of numerous immigrant languages and dialects entering the country after the establishment of the Republic make up a multi-stratified fourth layer. Stories of groups like the Irish, Germans, and Scandinavians in the mid-nineteenth century and the immigrants of the "Great Wave," entering the United States from 1880 to 1920, principally from China and southern and eastern European countries like Italy, Greece, Poland, and Czechoslovakia,[11] may hit close to home among students from regions that attracted large immigrant populations during the Industrial Revolution. Later immigration, particularly since 1965, and refugees from various countries under siege have added further diversity and complexity to the layering of languages and cultures in the United States. This material is highly adaptable and rich in terms of student engagement and discussion. Films abound, illustrating the immigrant experience with varying degrees of accuracy. To facilitate such interest, I ask my students to do research on their own family language histories—the language(s) of their heritages, including stories passed down or remembered. Even absence of information is considered "data" and can be included. Some students discover unknown ethnic backgrounds buried in family histories; many come in touch with legacies they did not know they had.

To emphasize the significance of social, political, and geographical context in language development from another perspective, I also draw a parallel between the history and experience of African American Language speakers and that of Hawai'i Creole English (HCE) speakers. While West Africans were brought to North American plantations enslaved and generally isolated from others who spoke the same languages to prevent insurrection, Asians from China, Japan, Korea, and the Philippines were brought to the Hawaiian Islands—along with thousands from Portugal and Puerto Rico, fewer from Norway, Germany, and other European countries (Takaki)—as contract labor and were segregated by language and ethnic group to discourage pan-ethnic resistance to harsh plantation conditions. In both situations, a White English-speaking oligarchy maintained positions of authority so that speakers of different native languages adapted to the English-speaking environments using pidgin English forms.[12] Pidgin English speakers and their creole-speaking descendants in both the Islands and the mainland United States have been stigmatized, especially with regard to education, although Dell Hymes referred to pidgin languages as "creative adaptations," epitomizing the very "interdependence of language and society" (3). In this regard, we discuss both Gilyard's codeswitching and the development of pidgin and creole forms as creative linguistic phenomena, exemplifying metalinguistic awareness, "verbal agility" (my term referring to the speaker's ability to interpret and move at will linguistically between varying social and rhetorical contexts), and the inherent relationships between language and identity.

Individual Language Histories: Students
Write Themselves into Awareness

In addition to sketching out the country's language history to illustrate the increasing complexity of U.S. multilingualism, I move the class to a microlevel study of individual linguistic and cultural acquisition—some basic language acquisition research—in this context of language varieties. In this way, students can begin to see the relationships between culture and language and between environment and linguistic behavior; they become familiar with the *universality* of the process, and the *particularity* of the circumstances, of acquiring the grammars (phonology, semantics, syntax, pragmatics) of any given language variety. As they learn how any child acquires language and develops communicative competence in different speech communities, they come to understand how inextricable culture and language are; as they see how they themselves become language users within a sociocultural context, they can appreciate more readily how this happens with others. Through this process, they may begin to see the validity of the linguists' claim that "everyone speaks a dialect" (Daniels 47–48).[13] Together with different theories of language acquisition, we discuss intersections of linguistic research and habitual, unexamined classroom practice related to the grammars of language, such as vocabulary study and grammar drills.[14] In an increasingly multilingual society, it is essential that preservice and in-service teachers alike become familiar with myths of grammar teaching and standardized English[15] and the cultural biases that are promoted by them. As Sledd points out, "[T]eachers must ask not just the surface questions of what rules to teach and when and how to teach and test them but the deeper questions of the nature and right purpose of the whole undertaking" ("Grammar for Social Awareness" 35).

Students of different ages and backgrounds can have some fun with discussions and activities concerning language varieties and practices influenced by geographical region, socioeconomic class, and gender. Again, films, audiotapes, websites, and, above all, students' personal observations are useful sources of examples. Although I show the PBS film *American Tongues* early in the course to introduce the relationship between language varieties and language attitudes, this video is equally useful in discussing geographical and class differences in language.

Providing students not only with conceptual tools but also with opportunities to reflect in writing on their own experiences, insights, and learning often encourages the "deeper questioning" and "deeper social awareness" that Sledd requests of us. As I illustrate

at greater length elsewhere (Okawa, "From 'Bad Attitudes'"), using language autobiographies and language logs allows students to
document their own family language histories and memories of personal language acquisition and development and to understand—
and assess—the origins of their own language attitudes. At some
point, students might realize how naturally they might become
ethnocentric through language and about language, depending on
the breadth of their exposure to different cultural environments. I
might also note that aspects of the instructor's background could
factor into such classroom discussions at different points; in this
regard, I find it useful to make my Asian appearance as a third-
generation Japanese American a kind of text of the class as a means
of instilling specific linguistic notions of language acquisition and of
exposing students' ethnocentricity to themselves. The cumulative
effect is usually a significant awakening for the students who experience it, as Jeanine's insight reveals:

> My attitudes have grown since I discovered and resurfaced
> the roots behind the closed minded attitudes. . . . As you
> resurface the roots of your language attitudes you can be-
> gin to change them. We grow up in an ethnocentric world
> and this is where we learn how to speak and develop our
> linguistic skills. I believe it is important to learn where
> your ethnocentric behavior stems from.

Other students, like Helen, refer more broadly to major epipha-
nies regarding the language varieties of others:

> This class has changed everything I once believed about
> Black English. I now see it with specific rules of grammar
> and its own unique system. The key I suppose is not to
> judge the language but to find a common place for when to
> use it. I am aware [that] I was very ethnocentric and felt
> like other people just did not understand "how to speak."
> After reading Gilyard and seeing the way his mom used
> codeswitching, I see that it simply is an issue of when to

use one's native language. All in all, because of the awareness this class has raised in me and the various authors
who dedicated their lives to bring language awareness to
people, I have changed beliefs I once held about Black English as well as language as a whole. I feel I can be a more
inspiring teacher because of this experience. . . . My value
judgements had to do with my parents, friends and teachers and just being ignorant [of] language's complexity.

Such insights are critical in future teachers and others developing
not only an awareness of their own language behavior but also a
sense of empathy and responsibility to respect the language varieties of others. They can then understand more readily the issues
raised in the CCCC "Students' Right to Their Own Language" resolution, written in 1974 to address questions of dialect variety, and
the CCCC National Language Policy, written two decades later to
express the current position of the profession on official language
legislation.

A Personal Recovery

In my opening paragraph, I mentioned having little appreciation
at one time for "Pidgin English," the regional vernacular of Hawai'i.
In a required freshman-level speech class in college, I remember
watching a Pidgin English–speaking classmate struggling to pronounce standardized English sounds and recall wincing in embarrassment for him. Like my African American student, who suffered
from "a shame born from a lack of knowledge regarding my history," I was painfully aware of the stigma associated with Hawai'i
Creole English but did not understand the complex sociolinguistic origins of the dialect nor the history of linguistic imperialism/
colonialism causing the shame that plagued its speakers.

After I left Honolulu for the East Coast, homesickness and occasional visits to Hawai'i during a burgeoning renaissance of local
culture led to my natural recovery of "Pidgin"[16] as not only my regional dialect but also a language of solidarity, of local identification

and pride. Much later, my graduate research on pidgins and creoles, together with the courageous publication by various Island writers of literature in Pidgin, have aided me greatly in this recovery process. It is enormously liberating. As I have come to reclaim my own home varieties and see this providing enrichment to my life and my classroom, I have also begun to ask different questions of myself and my colleagues in relation to home languages and the language of the academy.

Do You Speak My Language? A Pedagogical Proposal

In her 1993 article "Cultural Politics in the Academic Community: Masking the Color Line," Karla F. C. Holloway discusses the alarming resemblance between the world anticipated by W. E. B. DuBois in 1903 and that which we face in 2003, a century later—that condition described by DuBois as "the problem of the color line" (v). She warns us of the dangers of "one 'universal identity'" in academe, of masking our "diverse, subjective, biased, cultural, and decidedly political identities" in the face of it (614, 611). And she asserts that academics in this country must

> embrace to our own ends the identity politics—the perspectives of race, culture, gender, and ethnicity—inherent in language. We can claim the power of our voices, and their complexity, *and their complexions* to assert the dimensions of our concerns, to call attention to our successes in vitalizing the community of the university—both its faculty bodies and its student bodies. (617)

This is a critical charge for teachers of various linguistic and cultural backgrounds in the United States as we move into a new century with significantly different demographics from the last. And, I believe, it raises some interesting pedagogical questions for us, particularly in relation to *our* language use: for example, in what ways must academics—whose ethnic, cultural, and/or linguistic backgrounds differ greatly from that of the dominant European

American academic culture—transmigrate linguistically and rhetorically in coming to academe and the professoriate? Do we, metaphorically, leave one speaking body behind to step into one that functions successfully in the academic world? Traditionally, scholars have been expected to assimilate and master what some would call "the master's language." If we codeswitch (between or among different language varieties), what do we gain or lose? And if we don't, what do we gain or lose? In what ways, if any, do we transform the language of the academy, and how?

Transmigrations into Academe

At the risk of overgeneralizing and oversimplifying our experience, let me suggest a process that many of us might find familiar. Long before individuals seek "membership" in the academy, we as children may share the excitement of learning our home cultures and language(s) and naturally developing our identities through them, as linguistic studies in ethnicity and language document (for example, Edwards; Gee; Heath, *Ways with Words;* Van Horne) and as we know intuitively. In his mixed-genre autobiography, *Bootstraps: From an American Academic of Color,* Victor Villanueva Jr. portrays becoming not only bilingual in Spanish and English but also in many ways multidialectal in English as well. (He develops fluency in standardized English, Spanglish, and African American Language, the latter two varieties a product of growing up in a bilingual household and the projects of New York City). Such codeswitchers, whom Villanueva refers to as "rhetorical power players" (23), gain a complex metalinguistic command of language, which I termed "verbal agility" earlier in this chapter. In *Talking Back: Thinking Feminist, Thinking Black* bell hooks remembers "the world of woman talk" in her Southern Black community, one that instilled in her "the craving to speak, to have a voice, and not just any voice but one that could be identified as belonging to me" (5): "It was in this world of woman speech, loud talk, angry words, women with tongues quick and sharp, tender sweet tongues, touching our world with their words, that I made speech my birthright" (6).

Gloria Anzaldúa, in *Borderlands/La Frontera: The New Mestiza,* describes her fascination with language in childhood, reading "in bed with a flashlight under the covers" (65), making up stories for her sister so that she wouldn't tell on her. In her chapter "In Search of the Voice I Always Had," included in *The Leaning Ivory Tower: Latino Professors in American Universities*, María Cristina González narrates her early acquisition of cultural knowledge through the discourse of her Spanish-speaking family. And among the teachers of African American, Asian American, and Latino backgrounds who participated in a study that I conducted several years ago (Okawa, *Expanding Perspectives of Teacher Knowledge*), all were avid learners and creative users of language(s) in their home communities. Examples of verbal agility abound; they are all around and *in* us.

Often, encounters with schooling begin the process of imposed linguistic transmigration for speakers of such language varieties—at different points, for different reasons, in many cases caused by societal blows to self-esteem. hooks points out that "language is a crucial issue for folk whose movement outside the boundaries of poor and working-class backgrounds changes the nature and direction of their speech" (79). For example, Gilyard, in *Voices of the Self*, moves from Harlem to Queens and learns at an early age to succeed in a predominantly White school through codeswitching and identity-switching between two persona, one named Keith, the kid in the 'hood who speaks his native African American Language, and the other named Raymond, the successful student who speaks standardized English.

In another way, Villanueva, who had quite naturally learned to codeswitch among his various speech communities, who graduated third or fourth in his eighth grade class and even enjoyed spelling and parsing sentences, was denied entrance to the local college-prep high school and was sent to a vo-tech. Testing bias in language, he thinks now. Then he dropped out eventually, just short of graduating, when fulfillment of school aspirations seemed hopeless. Haunani-Kay Trask, in her book *From a Native Daughter: Colonialism and Sovereignty in Hawai'i*, describes conflicting stories about her Native Hawaiian people told by her parents and her boarding school teachers:

There was nothing in my schooling that had told me of this [her linguistic and historical heritage], or hinted that somewhere there was a longer, older story of origins, of the flowing of songs out to a great but distant sea. Only my parents' voices, over and over, spoke to me of a Hawaiian world. While the books spoke from a different world, a Western world. (154)

"By the time I left for college," she writes, "the books had won out over my parents, especially since I spent four long years in a missionary boarding school for Hawaiian children" (148). In Trask's experience, the cultural and linguistic erasure is in place from the outset of schooling; it is an implicit and insidious requirement of the educative process. Becoming literate in the school context means becoming socialized into the dominant culture, its language, its discourse, its version of history. We may be ignorant of our language history, or we may be forced to deny it in school. This process has its obvious costs; Gilyard calls them "psychic payments" (11).

In higher education, the problems may intensify; the payments required increase. The academy demands of its players objectivity, objectification, and, above all, uniformity in discourse and thought —Holloway's "universal identity" (614) and Villanueva's reference to "racelessness" (40). Assimilation. hooks describes this as "a static notion of self and identity that [is] pervasive in university settings" (11). In his autobiography, Villanueva portrays and analyzes his encounters with undergraduate and graduate school discourse. To the extent that he doesn't "get" the academic formulas, he fails but invents "Professorial Discourse Analysis" (71) as his survival skill. For González, it was in graduate school that she felt most alienated and uncomfortable:

The traditional indigenous, earth-based way of teaching that my grandfather used allowed me to learn principles implicitly, etching them indelibly into my character. Therefore, when I was confronted with new sets of "rules for being" in graduate school, the essence of the identity with which I was familiar, even if I was not conscious of it, was challenged. (81–82)

Regarding written discourse, González acknowledges having "excellent writing teachers, "who" encouraged me to express myself creatively" during elementary and secondary school and in college. "It was not until I was in graduate school that my creative voice began to be silenced in favor of orthodox modes and messages" (83–84). Through autobiographical narrative research, we can sometimes chart the shifts from one body to another.

Transforming the Language of School

Survivors of this process must become creative. And considering such issues of survival, I'd like to return to a question I asked earlier: In what ways, if any, do we academics of different ethnic, cultural, and/or linguistic backgrounds transform the language of school and the academy, and how? At one time, as Holloway points out in her essay, people like Gilyard, hooks, Villanueva, González, Trask, and some of us were the objects of academic study. Now, academically—they/we as insiders study and use the language and cultures of our communities and legitimate their existence not as aberrations of "parent" languages and cultures. Rather than perpetuating linguistic imperialist views, some scholars of Color make language a site of contestation and resistance. The linguistic and sociolinguistic work of scholars like Gilyard, Geneva Smitherman (*Talkin and Testifyin; Black Talk*), and John Baugh (*Black Street Speech*) on AAL reflects this, as does the work of the late Charlene Sato ("Linguistic Inequality in Hawai'i"; "A Nonstandard Approach to Standard English") on Hawai'i Creole English. Trask returned to Hawai'i with a Ph.D. in political science only to recognize her cultural loss, a recognition that instilled in her the desire to rectify this through a recovery of history and language:

> For so long, more than half my life, I had misunderstood [the] written record, thinking it described my own people. But my history was nowhere present. For we had not writ-

ten. . . . To know my history, I had to put away my books
and return to the land. I had to plant *taro* in the earth
before I could understand the inseparable bond between
people and *'aina*. . . . I had to begin to speak my language
with our elders and leave long silences for wisdom to grow.
But before anything else, I needed to learn the language
like a lover—so that I could rock within her and lie at night
in her dreaming arms. (154)

Individual studies of language like Smitherman's and Trask's have in
some cases led to institutional changes in curriculum and attitudes
toward language maintenance.

From a rhetorical perspective, we may choose and manipulate
forms of written discourse that afford us the opportunity to express ourselves, our lives, and the lives of our communities more
fully, through such forms as autobiography, narrative, theater, fiction, and poetry. Writers like Anzaldúa, Smitherman, Villanueva,
Darrell Lum, Toni Cade Bambara, Luci Tapahonso, Piri Thomas,
Lois-Ann Yamanaka, and others, who claim their ethnicities, cultures, and multiple languages and discourses, resist pressures to
write in "one way." In her article "The Englishes of Ethnic Folk:
From Home Talkin' to Testifyin' Art," Bonnie TuSmith discusses the
process by which "ethnic American writers develop various strategies for negotiating the space between their cultural experiences
and Anglo-American hegemony" where "the contest site is most
often the English language" (43). Such writers are less willing to
compromise their art for the intelligibility of what Linda Hogan
calls "the dominant and dominating world" (237). The transforma-
tion has been profound; as TuSmith asserts, "[B]y giving themselves
permission to incorporate their spoken language into the very structure of narration, such writers are, in effect, freeing American letters
to realize its rich potential" (55).

From a pedagogical perspective, we may theorize and teach using methods that allow for multiple cultural layers of expression
among our students. Smitherman's African American Language and
Literacy program at Michigan State University comes to mind; in

it, students of different ethnic backgrounds not only learn *about* AAL but also learn the language variety itself. hooks writes about her experiences of leaving Kentucky for Stanford and then graduate school and subsequent linguistic choices that she has made in her classrooms:

> Coming to Stanford with my own version of a Kentucky accent I learned to speak differently while maintaining the speech of my region, the sound of my family and community. . . . In recent years, I have endeavored to use various speaking styles in the classroom as a teacher and find it disconcerts those who feel that the use of a particular patois excludes them as listeners, even if there is translation into the usual, acceptable mode of speech. Learning to listen to different voices, hearing different speech challenges the notion that we must all assimilate—share a single, similar talk —in educational institutions. Language reflects the culture from which we emerge. To deny ourselves daily use of speech patterns that are common and familiar, that embody the unique and distinctive aspect of our self is one of the ways we become estranged and alienated from our past. (79)

So what about our *own* written and spoken discourse? Are scholars like Smitherman, Trask, and hooks exceptions or the rule? Have we changed the content but less so the spoken discourse of the academy? How extreme are the journeys we must make, must we continue to make? And how can we achieve a realistic multicultural form of language and literacy in higher education for ourselves and our increasing numbers of students of varying cultural and linguistic origins? Our cultures, languages, and identities are tightly interlocked within us as individuals. Don't the controversies on language varieties in schools thus logically extend to us in higher education? While language can become a point of alienation, it can also become a point of reconciliation and reunion—for the individual and the group. As hooks advises, we must truly change the nature of the academy, of its language and discourse. Otherwise, we make no room for the multiple voices of our students, we set no example for their variety in our own assimilation. How *do* we "embrace to our own ends . . . the perspectives of race, culture, gender, and ethnicity—inherent in language"? How do we "claim the power of our voices, and their complexity, *and their complexions*," as Holloway encourages us to do? How much do we require our students and colleagues to accommodate to our tongues? How often do we ask them to speak—at least understand—*our* languages?

If we claim language as our business, whatever our linguistic and cultural complexions may be, our pedagogy must reflect an awareness of the conditions around us—the multiplicity of language varieties in our communities, the rights of their speakers to maintain them in a democratic society, the forces endangering those rights. Becoming a part of global society makes our individual worlds more, not less, complex, more, not less, rich, but we must be made privy to the knowledge that would liberate us from our own provincialism and seclusion. One step, as my student Jeanine realizes, is to ferret out and examine the roots of that seclusion. Perhaps more than anyone else in society, teachers have the job—and power—to provide us with the knowledge to ask the questions, not in an isolated lesson plan but as a basis for our inquiry about the world. The study of language can not only yield the subject of that knowledge but also serve as the mechanism/method by which that knowledge is obtained. Rather than shrinking at the sounds of Pidgin English now, I long for the marketplace in Honolulu's Chinatown or Cleveland's West Side Market or Seattle's International District, where speakers of many languages and dialects willingly and necessarily negotiate their lives—across cultures and tongues. If only our classrooms could be as robust and healthy and natural.

Notes

Teaching and writing about teaching can never be a solitary activity. I would like to thank especially the students who have given me useful feedback on my language course throughout the years, H. Thomas McCracken with whom

I have discussed such matters as these for hours on end, and Victor Villanueva Jr., who makes time to read what I have to say.

1. Described by Robert Phillipson, Mart Rannut, and Tove Skutnabb-Kangas in their introduction to *Linguistic Human Rights: Overcoming Linguistic Discrimination* in the following terms:

> Observing LHRs implies at an *individual* level that everyone can iden-
> tify positively with their mother tongue, and have that identification
> respected by others, irrespective of whether their mother tongue is
> a minority language or a majority language . . . [and] at a *collective*
> level the right of minority groups to exist . . . to enjoy and develop
> their language and the right for minorities to establish and maintain
> schools and other training and educational institutions, with control
> of curricula and teaching in their own languages. (2)

See elaborated discussions on LHRs in the essays contained in this collection, especially "Language Policy in the United States: A History of Cultural Geno-cide," by Eduardo Hernández-Chávez.

2. See Phillipson, *Linguistic Imperialism*.

3. It should be noted that in these essays, reflection is solicited, but this kind of self-evaluation is not.

4. This topic is discussed at some length in my essay "From 'Bad Atti-tudes' To(wards) Linguistic Pluralism: Developing Reflective Language Policy among Preservice Teachers" in terms of the reflective writing of students.

5. A version of sections of the following text first appeared in Okawa, "From 'Bad Attitudes,'" in R. D. Gonzalez, ed., *Language Ideologies*.

6. See Molesky.

7. See Hernández-Chávez.

8. For an explanation of these terms, see Richard, Platt, and Weber's *Longman Dictionary of Applied Linguistics* and writings of Joshua A. Fishman, such as *Language and Ethnicity in Minority Sociolinguistic Perspective*.

9. See Hernández-Chávez; Molesky; Heath, "English in Our Language Heritage."

10. See Smitherman, *Talkin and Testifyin;* Dillard.

11. See Molesky.

12. See Dillard and Smitherman (1986) on historical background of Black English/AAL; see Carr, Reinecke, Sato, and Takaki on the development of Ha-wai'i Pidgin English and Hawai'i Creole English.

13. See also Wolfram, Adger, and Christian; Wolfram.

14. See the wealth of writings by linguists and educational researchers like Smith, Hartwell, Miller and Gildea, Cleary and Lund, and Sledd, which cri-tique rote and entrenched teaching methods.

15. Rather than the term "standard English," which conveys a universally

accepted standard, I prefer to use "standardized English," which implies political and social agency and is more historically accurate. See especially Cleary
and Lund; Hartwell; and Sledd, "Grammar for Social Awareness," on the teaching of grammar, as well as Gere and Smith; Heath, "English in Our Language
Heritage"; Sledd, "Standard English and the Study of Variations" and *Eloquent
Dissent;* Wolfram, Adger, and Christian; and *Students' Right to Their Own Language* on standardized English and dialects of American English.

16. See Okawa, "Resistance and Reclamation."

Works Cited

Anzaldúa, Gloria. *Borderlands/La Frontera: The New Mestiza.* San Francisco:
Spinsters/Aunt Lute, 1987.

Baugh, John. *Black Street Speech: Its History, Structure and Survival.* Austin: U of
Texas P, 1983.

"Black on White." *The Story of English* series. Dir./prod. William Cran. Chicago:
Films Inc.

Carr, Elizabeth. *Da Kine Talk: From Pidgin to Standard English in Hawaii.* Honolulu: UP of Hawaii, 1972.

CCCC Language Policy Committee. *Language Knowledge and Awareness Survey.*
Final Report. Jan. 2000 <http://www.ncte/org/cccc/langsurvey.pdf>.

———. *The National Language Policy.* Urbana, IL: NCTE, 1991 (brochure).

Cleary, Linda Miller, and Nancy Lund. "Debunking Some Myths about Traditional Grammar." *Linguistics for Teachers.* Ed. Linda Miller Cleary and
Michael D. Linn. New York: McGraw-Hill, 1993. 483–90.

Daniels, Harvey. "Nine Ideas About Language." *Language: Readings in Language
and Culture.* Ed. Virginia P. Clark, Paul A. Eschholz, and Alfred F. Rosa.
New York: St. Martin's, 1998. 43–60.

Dillard, J. L. *Black English: Its History and Usage in the United States.* New York:
Random, 1972.

DuBois, W. E. B. *The Souls of Black Folk.* 1903. New York: Dover, 1994.

Edwards, John. *Language, Identity, and Society.* New York: Blackwell, 1985.

Fishman, Joshua A. *Language and Ethnicity in Minority Sociolinguistic Perspective.* Philadelphia: Multilingual Matters, 1989.

Gee, James Paul. "The Narrativization of Experience in the Oral Style." *Rewriting Literacy: Culture and the Discourse of the Other.* Ed. Henry A. Giroux
and Paulo Freire. Toronto, Ont.: OISE P, 1991. 77–101.

Gere, Anne Ruggles, and Eugene Smith. *Attitudes, Language, and Change.* Urbana, IL: NCTE, 1979.

Gilyard, Keith. *Let's Flip the Script: An African American Discourse on Language,
Literature and Learning.* Detroit: Wayne State UP, 1996.

———. *Voices of the Self: A Study of Language Competence.* Detroit: Wayne State UP, 1991.

González, María Cristina. "In Search of a Voice I Always Had." *The Leaning Ivory Tower: Latino Professors in American Universities.* Ed. R. V. Padilla and R. C. Chávez. New York: State U of New York P, 1995. 77–90.

Hartwell, Patrick. "Grammar, Grammars, and the Teaching of Grammar." *College English* 47 (1985): 105–27.

Heath, Shirley Brice. "English in Our Language Heritage." *Language in the USA.* Ed. Charles A. Ferguson and Shirley Brice Heath. New York: Cambridge UP, 1981.

———. *Ways with Words: Language, Life, and Work in Communities and Classrooms.* New York: Cambridge UP, 1983.

Hernández-Chávez, Eduardo. "Language Policy in the United States: A History of Cultural Genocide." *Linguistic Human Rights: Overcoming Linguistic Discrimination.* Ed. Tove Skutnabb-Kangas and Robert Phillipson. New York: Mouton, 1994. 141–58.

Hogan, Linda. "The Two Lives." *I Tell You Now.* Ed. B. Swann and A. Krupat. Lincoln: U of Nebraska P, 1987. 231–49.

Holloway, Karla F. C. "Cultural Politics in the Academic Community: Masking the Color Line." *College English* 55.6 (1993): 610–17.

hooks, bell. *Talking Back: Thinking Feminist, Thinking Black.* Boston: South End P, 1989.

Hymes, Dell. Preface and introductions to sections. *Pidginization and Creolization of Languages.* Ed. Dell Hymes. New York: Cambridge UP, 1971.

Linkon, Sherry, and Bill Mullen. "Gender Race, and Place: Teaching Working-Class Students in Youngstown." *Radical Teacher* 46 (Spring 1995): 27–32.

Miller, George A., and Patricia M. Gildea. "How Children Learn Words." *Language: Readings in Language and Culture.* Ed. Virginia P. Clark, Paul A. Eschholz, and Alfred F. Rosa. New York: St. Martin's P, 1998. 580–87.

Molesky, Jean. "Understanding the American Linguistic Mosaic: A Historical Overview of Language Maintenance and Linguistic Shift." *Language Diversity: Problem or Resource?* Ed. Sandra Lee McKay and Sau-ling Cynthia Wong. New York: Newbury, 1987. 29–68.

Okawa, Gail Y. *Expanding Perspectives of Teacher Knowledge: A Descriptive Study of Autobiographical Narratives of Writing Teachers of Color.* Diss., Indiana U of Pennsylvania, 1995.

———. "From 'Bad Attitudes' To(wards) Linguistic Pluralism: Developing Reflective Language Policy among Preservice Teachers." *Education and the Social Implications of Official Language.* Ed. R. D. Gonzalez. Urbana, IL: NCTE, 2000. 276–96. Vol. 1 of *Language Ideologies: Critical Perspectives on the Official English Movement.* 2 vols. 2000–2001.

———. "Resistance and Reclamation: Hawaii's 'Pidgin English' and Autoethnography in the Short Stories of Darrell H. Y. Lum." *Ethnicity and the American Short Story.* Ed. J. Brown. New York: Garland, 1997. 177–96.

Okawa, Gail Y., and Elaine Richardson. "Seeds of Intolerance: Language Educators' Attitudes Towards Language and Dialect Diversity." Unpublished paper. CCCC Annual Convention, Minneapolis, MN, 2000.

Phillipson, Robert. *Linguistic Imperialism.* Oxford: Oxford UP, 1992.

Phillipson, Robert, Mart Rannut, and Tove Skutnabb-Kangas. Introduction. *Linguistic Human Rights: Overcoming Linguistic Discrimination.* Ed. Tove Skutnabb-Kangas and Robert Phillipson. New York: Mouton, 1994.

Reinecke, John. *Language and Dialect in Hawaii: A Sociolinguistic History to 1935.* Honolulu: U of Hawaii P, 1969.

Richards, J., J. Platt, and H. Weber. *Longman Dictionary of Applied Linguistics.* Essex, England: Longman, 1985.

Sato, Charlene J. "Linguistic Inequality in Hawai'i: The Post-Creole Dilemma." *Language of Inequality.* Ed. Nessa Wolfson and J. Manes. New York: Mouton, 1985. 255–72.

———. "A Nonstandard Approach to Standard English." *TESOL Quarterly* 23 (1989): 259–82.

Shaull, Richard. Foreword. *Pedagogy of the Oppressed.* By Paulo Freire. New York: Continuum, 1970.

Sledd, James. *Eloquent Dissent: The Writings of James Sledd.* Portsmouth, NH: Boynton, 1996.

———. "Grammar for Social Awareness in Time of Class Warfare." *English Journal* 85 (Nov. 1996): 35–39.

———. "Standard English and the Study of Variations: 'It All Be Done for a Purpose.'" *Language Variation in North American English.* Ed. A. W. Glowka and D. M. Lance. New York: MLA, 1993. 275–81.

Smith, Frank. *Understanding Reading: A Psycholinguistic Analysis of Reading and Learning to Read.* Hillsdale, NJ: Erlbaum, 1988.

Smitherman, Geneva. *Black Talk: Words and Phrases from the Hood to the Amen Corner.* New York: Houghton, 1994.

———. *Talkin and Testifyin: The Language of Black America.* Detroit: Wayne State UP, 1986.

Students' Right to Their Own Language. Spec. issue of *CCC* 25 (1974): 1–32.

Takaki, Ronald. *Pau Hana: Plantation Life and Labor in Hawaii.* Honolulu: U of Hawaii P, 1983.

Trask, Haunani-Kay. *From a Native Daughter: Colonialism and Sovereignty in Hawaii.* Monroe, ME: Common Courage P, 1993.

TuSmith, Bonnie. "The Englishes of Ethnic Folk: From Home Talkin' to Testifyin' Art." *College English* 58 (1996): 43–57.

Van Horne, Winston A., ed. *Ethnicity and Language.* Madison: U of Wisconsin System, 1987.

Villanueva, Victor. *Bootstraps: From an American Academic of Color.* Urbana, IL: NCTE, 1993.

Wolfram, Walt. "Everyone Has an Accent." *Teaching Tolerance* 18 (Fall 2000): 19–23.

Wolfram, Walt, Carolyn T. Adger, and Donna Christian. *Dialects in Schools and Communities.* Mahwah, NJ: Erlbaum, 1999.

7 / Language Diversity and the Classroom
Problems and Prospects, a Bibliography
C. Jan Swearingen and Dave Pruett

Some of the questions that emerge from this bibliography are how, where, and why many of the distinctions drawn between English language varieties and bilingualism have been shifting in the research conducted during the past decade. Are bidialectalism and bilingualism alike being subsumed under the banner of multiculturalism? How can a multicultural approach to language diversity be distinguished from a bidialectal or bilingual approach? In what circumstances should the divisions be collapsed, and when should they be maintained? The Ebonics debate can be seen as a watershed in this shift, for the Oakland Ebonics controversy brought to the surface long-simmering inequities in language policy and government funding that excluded African American students from funds available to bilingual student populations and programs. The same period saw a rising tide of English Only and anti-bilingual legislation, responses to increases in immigrant populations, but beneath that a return to older assimilationist attitudes.

Studies of White dialects have encouraged the incorporation of class and culture into studies of language diversity and have provided increasingly ample evidence of the overlaps between White and Black variants in the South and elsewhere. Spanish language bilingual and bidialectal studies distinguish Chicano/a, Hispanic, Latino/a, Puerto Rican, and Mexican American from one another. These are cultural as well as linguistic self-designations with political meanings inside and outside of the classroom, academia, and scholarship. All too few are studies of Native American bilingualism, education, and bidialectalism. History and demographics alike call for more studies in this area and more definition of the goals of

Native American studies, particularly in the unique case against as-similation that is embodied in Native American languages, histo-ries, and cultures.

Because of the rapidly diversifying developments in all these ar-eas of research, we have in most cases favored more recent over older publications. The newer publications include comprehensive bibliographies that provide access to the older works as well as access to the journals, some of them international, in which de-bates are currently being conducted. The titles and topics com-prised here make clear that parallels are being defined linking bi-dialectalism and bilingualism in ways that can dissolve some of the former boundaries. Once in school, bidialectal students and bi-lingual students face equally formidable encounters with a school culture unlike their home cultures. Many "remedial" classes ad-dress similar problems in White bidialectal English speaking stu-dents.

It is our intention in this compilation to reflect present patterns in research on language diversity and to encourage more studies and new methodologies. In addition to fostering combined studies of bilingualism and bidialectalism that can help us understand their parallels and not simply their differences, many recent studies also advocate a more carefully defined role for linguists in the classroom. How can descriptive linguistics and sociolinguistics, highly tolerant and protective of language variation, help define pedagogies for classrooms teaching a standard common language? Should class-rooms emphasize or require a common language? What, if any, are the limits of pluralism? The research studies that follow should help in answering such questions.

The topics are arranged in the following order:

Research Resources, Old and New
Bilingualism: Language Diversity General Studies
African American Language and Cultures
Asian American Cultures and Languages
Native American Languages, Cultures, and Education Policy
Spanish Languages, Cultures, Bilingualism, and Bidialectalism

Research Resources, Old and New

Baugh, John. *Beyond Ebonics: Linguistic Pride and Racial Prejudice.* New York: Oxford UP, 2000.

———. *Out of the Mouths of Slaves: African American Language and Educational Malpractice.* Austin: U of Texas P, 1999. Continuing recent work by a premier sociolinguist and African Americanist. Relentless, detailed focus on defining racism inside and outside educational settings; solutions suggested with more precision than many linguistic studies provide, particularly for education. Ample bibliography and suggestions for further research.

Bernstein, Basil. *Class, Codes, and Control.* London: Routledge, 1973. Classic kickoff for many subsequent studies of class and language. Invites discussion of differences between British and U.S. class and language practices.

Crawford, James, ed. *Language Loyalties: A Source Book on the Official English Controversy.* Chicago: U of Chicago P, 1992. Overview essays on U.S. and international language policy past and present, minority language rights, education, and symbolism of disputes about English Only. Very good range of languages and ethnicities, with specific chapters on demographics and court cases and school and school board disputes.

Dudley-Marling, Curt, and Carol Edelsky, eds. *The Fate of Progressive Language Policies and Practices.* Urbana, IL: NCTE, 2001. Part 1: historical and theoretical background. Part 2: local activism, reports from the field. Up-to-date surveys and case studies provide a wealth of information on individual projects. Historical and theoretical materials well selected for general reader and nonspecialist.

Fishman, Joshua. *The Rise and Fall of the Ethnic Revival: Perspectives on Language and Ethnicity.* Berlin: Mouton, 1985. Renowned international scholar working in the areas of language change, bilingualism and bilingual education, language policy, and sociology of language and of education policy. Anything by Fishman is valuable; this study focuses on a middle period in identity politics tied to language and education policy. Detailed bibliography.

Gilyard, Keith. *Let's Flip the Script: An African American Discourse on Language, Literature, and Learning.* Detroit: Wayne State UP, 1996.

———. *Race, Rhetoric, and Composition.* Portsmouth, NH: Boynton, 1999. Comprehensive assessments of race, culture, and classroom as well as social issues. Displays as well as depicts language variation and language and identity issues. Excellent bibliography and methodological models for further inquiry. As in his earlier *Voice of the Self,* Gilyard here develops models for pluralist language policy and pedagogy, moving beyond assimilationism and bidialectalism. Valuable bibliographical resources throughout.

González, Roseann Dueñas, and Ildikó Melis, eds. *Language Ideologies: Critical*

Perspectives on the Official English Movement. 2 vols. Mahwah, NJ: Erlbaum, 2001. Vol. 1: *Education and the Social Implications of Official Language.* Vol. 2: *History, Theory, and Policy.* Current state of debates and practices that affect bilingual education. Ties to multicultural and bidialectal studies of language variation and public attitudes toward diversity and pedagogy. Especially valuable for teachers working with parent groups who are divided over bilingual education, ESL, and remedial approaches to bidialectalism. Thorough, detailed bibliography.

Gumperz, John J., and Stephen Levinson, eds. *Rethinking Linguistic Relativity.* Cambridge: Cambridge UP, 1996. Reprise of thirty years of research on language and social status, language change, diglossia, and class and language. Asks linguists to rethink their neutrality on issues of language diversity.

Heath, Shirley Brice. "Protean Shapes in Literacy Events: Ever-Shifting Oral and Literate Tendencies." *Spoken and Written Language.* Ed. Deborah Tannen. Norwood, NJ: Ablex, 1982. 91–117. Spoken and written vernaculars.

———. *Ways with Words: Language, Life, and Work in Communities and Classrooms.* New York: Cambridge UP, 1983. Heath's work pioneered methodologies for comparative studies of adjacent linguistic communities and their interactions with one another inside and outside schools. Her study of Appalachian rural Whites documents the poor preparation of non-mainstream Whites for schooling, albeit for reasons different from their African American neighbors. Sociolinguistic analysis of teacher language and teacher-student interactions provide valuable documentation of failed classroom communication and suggests remedies. Ample bibliography; detailed footnotes.

Labov, William. "The Logic of Non-Standard English." *Language and Social Context.* Ed. Pier Paolo Giglioli. Harmondsworth, England: Penguin, 1972.

———. *The Social Stratification of English in New York City.* Washington, DC: Center for Applied Linguistics, 1972. Early U.S. studies of class, race, and language variation. Useful for comparison with methods used today to study ethnicity and language and pedagogical versus social issues related to ethnicity and language.

Orfield, Gary, Richard D. Kahlenberg, Edmund W. Gordon, Fred Genesee, Paul D. Slocumb, and Ruby K. Payne. "The New Diversity." *Principal* 79.5 (2000): 6–32. In this special issue, various authors (in separate articles) discuss the new face of school segregation; socioeconomic integration—a plan to mix poor and middle-class students; and ways to bridge the achievement gap between White students and students of Color, teach linguistically diverse students, and identify and nurture the gifted poor.

Parks, Stephen. *Class Politics: The Movement for the Students' Right to Their Own Language.* Foreword by Richard Ohmann. Urbana, IL: NCTE, 2000. Historical study of the contexts for the still-controversial 1974 "Students'

Right" statement. Emphasizes ties to present day discussions of Ebonics, dialects, class-related English variants, and bilingual education. Useful to compare with history depicted in chapter 1 of this volume.

Reyhner, Jon, Joseph Martin, Louise Lockard, and W. Sakiestewa Gilbert, eds. *Learn in Beauty: Indigenous Education for a New Century*. Flagstaff: Northern Arizona UP, 2000. A welcome, able contribution to the study of Native American languages; Native American bilingualism, bidialectalism, and biculturalism; and language and education policy past and present.

Smitherman, Geneva. *Black Talk: Words and Phrases from the Hood to the Amen Corner*. Boston: Houghton, 2000.

———. *Talkin and Testifyin: The Language of Black America*. Detroit: Wayne State UP, 1986.

———. *Talkin That Talk: Language, Culture, and Education in African America*. New York: Routledge, 2000. Influential, widely acclaimed groundbreakers in African American Language studies. Special attention to schooling at all levels and among different socioeconomic groups illustrates pervasiveness of racism. Detailed accounts of identity politics and crisis of self-identification through language, leading to school English being associated with whiteness by many African American youth.

Villanueva, Victor. *Bootstraps: From an American Academic of Color*. Urbana, IL: NCTE, 1993. Well-received study of Puerto Rican culture in the United States. Detailed description in this literacy narrative clarifies the differences among U.S. Latino/a populations and illustrates class, ethnicity, and national origin issues that overlap language in identity politics and educational success. Like Keith Gilyard, Villanueva outlines a program for pluralist pedagogy that can move beyond earlier assimilationist and bidialectal pedagogies. Detailed bibliography.

Wardhaugh, Ronald. *An Introduction to Sociolinguistics*. 3rd ed. Malden, MA: Blackwell, 1998. Accessible overview for nonspecialists. Ample, up-to-date bibliography. Chapters concentrate on the history and present state of major fields within sociolinguistics: language and dialect varieties, pidgins and creoles, codeswitching, speech communities, regional and social variants, language change, language and culture, ethnography, solidarity and politeness, speech acts and conversation, language and gender, language and disadvantage, language planning.

Wolfram, Walt. *Dialects and American English*. Englewood Cliffs, NJ: Prentice, 1991.

Wolfram, Walt, and Ralph Fasold. *The Study of Social Dialects in American English*. Englewood Cliffs, NJ: Prentice, 1974. Then and now studies by one of the deans of American dialect studies. The demarcations of region and social class and the relations of dialect to education are traced in different ways in the two studies but always with illuminating detail and engaging humor. Invites consideration of how dialects have been romanticized, exoticized, and othered by linguists as much as by literary authors, sometimes to the practical detriment of their speakers.

Bilingualism: Language Diversity General Studies

Allred, Alexandra, and Karen Powe. "If You Speak Two Languages, You Are Bilingual. If You Speak One Language, You Are American." *Updating School Board Policies* 25.1 (1994): 1–4.

Anderson, Peggy J. "Language Variation in the United States: Untangling the Issues." *Multicultural Education* 3.4 (1996): 8–11.

Angelova, Maria, and Anastasia Riazantseva. "'If You Don't Tell Me, How Can I Know?' A Case Study of Four International Students Learning to Write the U.S. Way." *Written Communication* 16 (1999): 491–525.

Aranowitz, Stanley, and Henry Giroux. *Education under Siege: The Conservative, Liberal, and Radical Debate over Schooling.* South Hadley, MA: Bergin, 1985.

Baker, Colin, and Sylvia Prys Jones. *Encyclopedia of Bilingualism and Bilingual Education.* Clevedon, England: Multilingual Matters, 1998.

Balhorn, Mark. "Paper Representations of the Non-Standard Voice." *Visible Language* 32 (1998): 56–74.

Barter, Richard. "Multiculturalism and Multilingualism: What It Means in Practice." *International Schools Journal* 27 (Spring 1994): 31–40.

Beykont, Zeynep F., ed. *Lifting Every Voice: Pedagogy and Politics of Bilingualism.* Cambridge, MA: Harvard Education Publishing Group, 2000.

Breton, Roland. "The Dynamics of Ethnolinguistic Communities as the Central Factor in Language Policy and Planning." *International Journal of the Sociology of Language* 118 (1996): 163–79.

Carranza, Isolda. "Multilevel Analysis of Two-Way Immersion Classroom Discourse." *Georgetown University Round Table on Languages and Linguistics* (1995): 169–87.

Cary, Stephen. *Working with Second Language Learners: Answers to Teachers' Top Ten Questions.* Portsmouth, NH: Heinemann, 2000.

Christian, Donna. "Language Development in Two-Way Immersion: Trends and Prospects." *Georgetown University Round Table on Languages and Linguistics* (1996): 30–42.

Clark, Ellen Riojas, et al. "Language and Culture: Critical Components of Multicultural Teacher Education." *Urban Review* 28.2 (1996): 185–97.

Combs, Mary Carol. "Public Perceptions of Official English/English Only: Framing the Debate in Arizona." *Sociopolitical Perspectives on Language Policy and Planning in the USA.* Ed. Thom Huebner and Kathryn A. Davis. Amsterdam: Benjamins, 1999. 131–54.

Crawford, James. *At War with Diversity: U.S. Language Policy in an Age of Anxiety.* Clevedon, England: Multilingual Matters, 2000.

Crystal, David. "The Future of Englishes." *English Today* 15.2 (1999): 10–20.

De Varennes, Fernand. "Law, Language and the Multiethnic State." *Language and Communication* 16 (1996): 291–300.

Dicker, Susan J. "Adaptation and Assimilation: U.S. Business Responses to Linguistic Diversity in the Workplace." *Journal of Multilingual and Multicultural Development* 19 (1998): 282–302.

———. *Languages in America: A Pluralist View*. Clevedon, England: Multilingual Matters, 1996.

Flexner, Stuart Berg, and Anne H. Soukhanov. *Speaking Freely: A Guided Tour of American English from Plymouth Rock to Silicon Valley*. New York: Oxford UP, 1997.

Hairston, Maxine. "Diversity, Ideology, and Teaching Writing." *CCC* 43 (1992): 179–93.

Hakuta, Kenji, and Elizabeth Feldman Mostafapour. "Perspectives from the History and Politics of Bilingualism and Bilingual Education in the United States." *Cultural and Language Diversity and the Deaf Experience*. Ed. Ila Parasnis. Cambridge: Cambridge UP, 1996. 38–50.

Hall, Joan Kelly, and William G. Eggington, eds. *The Sociopolitics of English Language Teaching*. Clevedon, England: Multilingual Matters, 2000.

Johnson, Fern L. *Speaking Culturally: Language Diversity in the United States*. Thousand Oaks, CA: Sage, 2000.

Johnstone, Barbara, and Judith Mattson Bean. "Self-Expression and Linguistic Variation." *Language in Society* 26.2 (1997): 221–46.

Kondo, Kimi. "The Paradox of U.S. Language Policy and Japanese Language Education in Hawai'i." *International Journal of Bilingual Education and Bilingualism* 1 (1998): 47–64.

Krauss, Michael. "The Condition of Native North American Languages: The Need for Realistic Assessment and Action." *International Journal of the Sociology of Language* 132 (1998): 9–21.

Lippi-Green, Rosina. *English with an Accent: Language, Ideology, and Discrimination in the United States*. London: Routledge, 1997.

Macedo, Donaldo. "The Colonialism of the English Only Movement." *Educational Research* 29.3 (2000): 15–24.

———. "The Illiteracy of English-Only Literacy." *Educational Leadership* 57.4 (Dec. 1999–Jan. 2000): 62–67.

Muysken, Pietr. *Bilingual Speech, a Typology of Code Switching*. Cambridge: Cambridge UP, 2002.

Phillipson, Robert, ed. *Rights to Language: Equity, Power, and Education*. Mahwah, NJ: Erlbaum, 2000.

Siegel, Jeff. "Stigmatized and Standardized Varieties in the Classroom: Interference or Separation?" *TESOL Quarterly* 33 (1999): 701–28.

Silva, Tony, and Paul Kei Matsuda, eds. *On Second Language Writing*. Mahwah, NJ: Erlbaum, 2001.

Simich-Dudgeon, Carmen, and Timothy Boals. "Language and Education Policy in the State of Indiana: Implications for Language Minority Students." *TESOL Quarterly* 30 (1996): 537–55.

Sledd, Andrew E. "Pigs, Squeals and Cow Manure or Power, Language and Multi-cultural Democracy." *Journal of Advanced Composition* 14.2 (1994): 547–48.

Sledd, James. "Doublespeak: Dialectology in the Service of Big Brother." *Black Language Reader*. Ed. R. H. Bentley and S. D. Crawford. Glenview, IL: Scott, 1973. 191–214.

Smith, Howard L. "Bilingualism and Bilingual Education: The Child's Perspective." *International Journal of Bilingual Education and Bilingualism* 2.4 (1999): 268–81.

Students' Right to Their Own Language. Spec. issue of *CCC* 25 (1974): 1–32.

African American Language and Cultures

Akintunde, Omowale. "Rap, Race, and Ebonics: The Effect of EPD (European Paradigm Domination) and Visual Media on American Education and Formulation of Social Values." *Griot: Official Journal of the Southern Conference on Afro-American Studies, Inc.* 17 (1998): 20–31.

Bailey, Guy, and Jan Tillery. "The Persistence of Southern American English." *Journal of English Linguistics* 24 (1996): 308–21.

Balester, V. M. *Cultural Divide: A Study of African-American College-Level Writers*. Portsmouth, NH: Boynton, 1993.

Ball, A., and T. Lardner. "Dispositions Toward Language: Teacher Constructs of Knowledge and the Ann Arbor Black English Case." *CCC* 48 (1997): 469–85.

Ball, Arnetha F. "Expository Writing of African American Students." *English Journal* 85.1 (1996): 27–36.

Baron, Dennis. "Ebonics and the Politics of English." *World Englishes* 19 (2000): 5–19.

———. "Ebonics Is Not a Panacea for Students at Risk." *Chronicle of Higher Education* 24 Jan. 1997: B4–B6.

Baugh, John. *Beyond Ebonics: Linguistic Pride and Racial Prejudice*. New York: Oxford UP, 2000.

———. *Black Street Speech*. Austin: U of Texas P, 1983.

Benedicto, Elena, Lamya Abdulkarim, Debra Garrett, Valerie Johnson, and Harry N. Seymour. "Overt Copulas in African American English Speaking Children." *Proceedings of the Boston University Conference on Language Development* 22 (1998): 50–57.

Blake, Renée. "Defining the Envelope of Linguistic Variation: The Case of 'Don't Count' Forms in the Copula Analysis of African American Vernacular English." *Language Variation and Change* 9.1 (1997): 57–79.

Burling, Robbins. *English in Black and White*. New York: Holt, 1973.

Collins, M., and C. Tamarkin. *Marva Collins' Way*. Los Angeles: Tarcher, 1982.

Dillard, J. L. *Black English: Its History and Usage in the United States*. New York: Random, 1972.

Fasold, Ralph W., and Yoshiko Nakano. "Contraction and Deletion in African American Vernacular English: Creole History and Relationship to Euro-American English." *Variation and Change in Language and Society*. Ed. Gregory R. Guy, Crawford Feagin, Deborah Schiffrin, and John Baugh. Vol. 1 of *Towards a Social Science of Language: Papers in Honor of William Labov*. Amsterdam: Benjamins, 1996. 373–95.

Feigenbaum, Irwin. "The Use of Nonstandard English in Teaching Standard: Contrast and Comparison." *Teaching Standard English in the Inner City*. Ed. R. W. Fasold and R. W. Shuy. Washington, DC: Center for Applied Linguistics, 1970. 87–104.

Gadsden, V. *Literacy among African American Youth: Issues in Learning, Teaching, and Schooling*. Cresskill, NJ: Hampton, 1995.

Gilyard, Keith. *Voices of the Self: A Study of Language Competence*. African American Life Series. Detroit: Wayne State UP, 1991.

Gundaker, Grey. *Signs of Diaspora/Diaspora of Signs: Literacies, Creolization, and Vernacular Practice in African America*. New York: Oxford UP, 1997.

Harris, Joyce L., Alan G. Kamhi, and Karen E. Pollock, eds. *Literacy in African American Communities*. Mahwah, NJ: Erlbaum, 2001.

Holloway, J. E. *The African Heritage of American English*. Bloomington: Indiana UP, 1993.

Hoover, Mary Rhodes. "A Recommended Reading List for Teachers of Students Who Speak Ebonics." *Journal of Negro Education* 67 (1998): 43–47.

Howard, Rebecca Moore. "The Great Wall of African American Vernacular English in the American College Classroom." *Journal of Advanced Composition (JAC): A Journal of Composition Theory* 16 (1996): 265–83.

Kochman, T. *Black and White Styles in Conflict*. Chicago: U of Chicago P, 1981.

———, ed. *Rappin' and Stylin' Out: Communication in Urban Black America*. Urbana/Champaign: U of Illinois P, 1972.

Linguistics and Education 7.1–2 (1995): 1–156. Spec. issues on Africanized English and education.

Linnes, Kathleen. "Middle-Class AAVE versus Middle-Class Bilingualism: Contrasting Speech Communities." *American Speech* 73 (1998): 339–67.

Middleton, Joyce Irene. "Back to Basics, or, the Three R's: Race, Rhythm, and Rhetoric." *Teaching English in the Two-Year College* 21.2 (1994): 104–13.

Miller, John J. "English Is Broken Here." *Policy Review* 79 (1996): 54–55.

Mufwene, Salikoko S., John Rickford, Guy Baley, and John Baugh, eds. *African-American English: Structure, History, and Use*. New York: Routledge, 1998.

Ogbu, John U. "Beyond Language: Ebonics, Proper English, and Identity in a Black-American Speech Community." *American Educational Research Journal* 36 (1999): 147–84.

Richardson, Elaine. "The Anti-Ebonics Movement: 'Standard' English Only." *Journal of English Linguistics* 26 (1998): 156–69.

Rickford, John R. "The Ebonics Controversy in My Backyard: A Sociolinguist's Experiences and Reflections." *Journal of Sociolinguistics* 3 (1999): 267–75.

———. "Prior Creolization of African-American Vernacular English? Socio-historical and Textual Evidence from the 17th and 18th Centuries." *Journal of Sociolinguistics* 1 (1997): 315–36.

Smitherman, Geneva, ed. *Black English and the Education of Black Children and Youth: Proceedings of the National Invitational Symposium on the King Decision.* Detroit: Center for Black Studies, Wayne State UP, 1981.

———. "Black English: Diverging or Converging? The View from the National Assessment of Educational Progress." *Language and Education* 6.1 (1992): 47–61.

———. "'The Blacker the Berry the Sweeter the Juice': African American Student Writers." *The Need for Story: Cultural Diversity in Classroom and Community.* Ed. A. H. Dyson and C. Genishi. Urbana, IL: NCTE, 1994. 80–101.

———. "'What Go Round': King in Perspective." *Harvard Educational Review* 51.1 (1981): 40–56.

Smitherman, Geneva, and Sylvia Cunningham. "'Dat Teacher Be Hollin At Us'— What Is Ebonics?" *TESOL Quarterly* 32 (1998): 139–43.

———. "Ebonics, *King,* and Oakland: Some Folk Don't Believe Fat Meat Is Greasy." *Journal of English Linguistics* 26 (1998): 97–107.

———. "Moving Beyond Resistance: Ebonics and African American Youth." *Journal of Black Psychology* 23 (1997): 227–32.

Taylor, Orlando L. "Ebonics and Educational Policy: Some Issues for the Next Millennium." *Journal of Negro Education* 67 (1998): 35–42.

Watson, Clifford, and Geneva Smitherman. *Educating African American Males: Detroit's Malcolm X Academy Solution.* Chicago: Third World, 1996.

Williams, R. L. "The Ebonics Controversy." *Journal of Black Psychology* 23 (1997): 208–14.

———, ed. *Ebonics: The True Language of Black Folks.* St. Louis: Institute for Black Studies, 1975.

Winford, Donald. "On the Origins of African American Vernacular English—A Creolist Perspective, I: The Sociohistorical Background." *Diachronica* 14 (1997): 305–44.

———. "On the Origins of African American Vernacular English—A Creolist Perspective, II: Linguistic Features." *Diachronica* 15 (1998): 99–154.

Wolfram, W., and R. W. Fasold. "Dialect Awareness and the Study of Language." *Students as Researchers of Culture and Language in Their Own Communities.* Ed. Ann Egan-Robertson and David Bloome. Cresskill, NJ: Hampton, 1998. 167–90.

———. "Toward Reading Materials for Speakers of Black English: Three Linguistically Appropriate Passages." *Teaching Black Children to Read.* Ed.

J. C. Baratz and R. W. Shuy. Washington, DC: Center for Applied Linguistics, 1969. 138–55.

Woodford, M. "The Black Scholar Reader's Forum on Ebonics." *Black Scholar* 27.1 (1997): 2–3.

Wright, Richard L. *Black Boy: A Record of Childhood and Youth.* New York: Harper, 1966.

———. "Sociolinguistic and Ideological Dynamics of the Ebonics Controversy." *Journal of Negro Education* 67 (1998): 5–15.

Asian American Cultures and Languages

Cheung, Him, and Hsuan-chih Chen. "Lexical and Conceptual Processing in Chinese-English Bilinguals: Further Evidence for Asymmetry." *Memory and Cognition* 26 (1998): 1002–13.

Ching, Marvin K. L., and Hsiang-te Kung. "Ethnic Identity, Americanization, and Survival of the Mother Tongue: The First-vs. the Second-Generation Chinese of Professionals in Memphis." *Language Variety in the South Revisited.* Ed. Cynthia Bernstein, Thomas Nunnally, and Robin Sabino. Tuscaloosa: U of Alabama P, 1997. 163–70.

Lo, Adrienne. "Heteroglossia and the Construction of Asian American Identities." *Issues in Applied Linguistics* 8 (1997): 47–62.

Mouw, Ted, and Yu Xie. "Bilingualism and the Academic Achievement of First- and Second-Generation Asian Americans: Accommodation with or Without Assimilation?" *American Sociological Review* 64 (1999): 232–52.

Xia, Ningsheng. "Maintenance of the Chinese Language in the United States." *The Bilingual Review/La revista bilingue* 17.3 (1992): 195–209.

Yoon, Keumsil Kim. "A Case Study of Fluent Korean-English Bilingual Speakers: Group Membership and Code Choices." *Journal of Pragmatics* 25 (1996): 395–407.

Young, Russell, and Myluong Tran. "Language Maintenance and Shift among Vietnamese in America." *International Journal of the Sociology of Language* 140 (1999): 77–82.

Native American Languages, Cultures, and Education Policy

Batchelder, Ann. "Teaching Dine' Language and Culture in Navajo Schools: Voices from the Community." Reyhner, Martin, Lockard, and Gilbert 1–8.

Bielenberg, Brian. "Charter Schools for American Indians." Reyhner, Martin, Lockard, and Gilbert 132–51.

Dick, Galena Sells. "I Maintained a Strong Belief in My Language and Culture: A Navajo Language Autobiography." *International Journal of the Sociology of Language* 132 (1998): 23–25.

Fillerup, Michael. "Racing Against Time: A Report on the Leupp Navajo Immersion Project." Reyhner, Martin, Lockard, and Gilbert 21–34.

Goodluck, Mary Ann, Louise Lockard, and Darlene Yazzie. "Language Revitalization in Navajo/English Dual Language Classrooms." Reyhner, Martin, Lockard, and Gilbert 9–20.

Greymorning, Stephen. "Observations on Response Towards Indigenous Cultural Perspectives as Paradigms in the Classroom." Reyhner, Martin, Lockard, and Gilbert 71–84.

Halmari, Helena. "Language Maintenance on the Alabama-Coushatta Reservation." *Anthropological Linguistics* 40.3 (1998): 409–28.

Jeanne, LaVerne Masayesva. "An Institutional Response to Language Endangerment: A Proposal for a Native American Language Center." *Language* 68 (1992): 24–28.

Krauss, Michael. "The Condition of Native North American Languages: The Need for Realistic Assessment and Action." *International Journal of the Sociology of Language* 132 (1998): 9–21.

Lockard, Louise. "We Could Make a Book: The Textual Tradition of Navajo Language Literacy 1940–1990." *Southwest Journal of Linguistics* 17 (1998): 99–107.

McCarty, Teresa L. "Schooling, Resistance, and American Indian Languages." *International Journal of the Sociology of Language* 132 (1998): 27–41.

Reyhner, Jon, Joseph Martin, Louise Lockard, and W. Sakiestewa Gilbert, eds. *Learn in Beauty: Indigenous Education for a New Century.* Flagstaff: Northern Arizona UP, 2000.

Richardson, Louise Barbara. "The Development of the Lakota-English Bilingual Program on the Rosebud Reservation." *Language and Communication in the New Century.* Ed. Jesse Levitt, Leonard R. N. Ashley, and Wayne H. Finke. Proc. of a Conference of the American Society of Geolinguistics in Association with the City University of New York Academy of Humanities and Sciences, 16–17 Oct. 1997. New York: Cummings and Hathaway, 1998. 167–78.

———. "Tribal College Curricula as Evidence for the Contemporary Use of Indigenous Languages in North America." *Geolinguistics* 23 (1997): 61–77.

Zepeda, Ofelia, and Jane H. Hill. "The Condition of Native American Languages in the United States." *Endangered Languages.* Ed. Robert H. Robins and Eugenius M. Uhlenbeck. Oxford: Berg, 1991. 135–55.

Spanish Languages, Cultures, Bilingualism, and Bidialectalism

Barrera, Mario. *Race and Class in the Southwest: A Theory of Racial Inequality.* Notre Dame, IN: U of Notre Dame P, 1979.

Bartolome, Lilia I., and Donaldo Macedo. "(Mis)Educating Mexican Americans Through Language." *Sociopolitical Perspectives on Language Policy and Planning in the USA*. Ed. Thom Huebner and Kathryn A. Davis. Amsterdam: Benjamins, 1999. 223–41.

Bayley, Robert, and Lucinda Pease-Alvarez. "Null Pronoun Variation in Mexican-Descent Children's Narrative Discourse." *Language Variation and Change* 9 (1997): 349–71.

Bloom, David E., and Gilles Grenier. "Language, Employment, and Earnings in the United States: Spanish-English Differentials from 1970 to 1990." *International Journal of the Sociology of Language* 121 (1996): 45–68.

Brisk, María Estela. *Bilingual Education: From Compensatory to Quality Schooling*. Mahwah, NJ: Erlbaum, 1998.

Carrasquillo, Angela, and Philip Segan, eds. *The Teaching of Reading in Spanish to the Bilingual Student/La Enseñanza de la Lectura en Español para el Estudiante Bilingüe*. 2nd ed. Mahwah, NJ: Erlbaum, 1998.

Coles, Felice Anne. "The Isleno Dialect of Spanish: Language Maintenance Strategies." *Sociolinguistics of the Spanish-Speaking World: Iberia, Latin America, United States*. Ed. Carol A. Klee and Luis A. Ramos-Garcia. Tempe, AZ: Bilingual/Bilingue, 1991. 312–28.

D'Introno, Francesco. "Spanish-English Code-Switching: Conditions on Movement." *Spanish in Contact: Issues in Bilingualism*. Ed. Ana Roca and John B. Jensen. Somerville, MA: Cascadilla, 1996. 187–201.

Ebsworth, Miriam Eisenstein, and Timothy Ebsworth. "The Pragmatics and Perceptions of Multicultural Puerto Ricans." *International Journal of the Sociology of Language* 142 (2000): 119–55.

Francis, Wendy S. "Analogical Transfer of Problem Solutions Within and Between Languages in Spanish-English Bilinguals." *Journal of Memory and Language* 40.3 (1999): 301–29.

Galindo, D. Letticia. "Calo and Taboo Language Use among Chicanas: A Description of Linguistic Appropriation and Innovation." *Speaking Chicana: Voice, Power, and Identity*. Ed. D. Letticia Galindo and Maria Dolores Gonzales. Tucson: U of Arizona P, 1999. 175–93.

———. "A Sociolinguistic Study of Spanish Language Maintenance and Linguistic Shift Towards English among Chicanos." *Lenguas Modernas* 18 (1991): 107–16.

Garcia, Ofelia. "Spanish Language Loss as a Determinant of Income among Latinos in the United States: Implications for Language Policy in Schools." *Power and Inequality in Language Education*. Ed. James W. Tollefson. Cambridge: Cambridge UP, 1995. 142–60.

Jaramillo, June A. "The Passive Legitimization of Spanish: A Macrosociolinguistic Study of a Quasi-Border: Tucson, Arizona." *International Journal of the Sociology of Language* 114 (1995): 67–91.

Jimenez, Robert T., and Russell Gersten. "Lessons and Dilemmas Derived from the Literacy Instruction of Two Latina/o Teachers." *American Educational Research Journal* 36.2 (1999): 265–301.

Kalmar, Tomás Mario. *Illegal Alphabets and Adult Biliteracy: Latino Migrants Crossing the Linguistic Border*. Mahwah, NJ: Erlbaum, 2001.

King, Robert D. "Lessons of Public Linguistics." *Southwest Journal of Linguistics* 18.1 (1999): 1–14.

MacSwan, Jeff. "The Threshold Hypothesis, Semilingualism, and Other Contributions to a Deficit View of Linguistic Minorities." *Hispanic Journal of Behavioral Sciences* 22.1 (2000): 3–45.

Morris, Nancy. "Language and Identity in Twentieth-Century Puerto Rico." *Journal of Multilingual and Multicultural Development* 17 (1996): 17–32.

Murguia, Edward. *Assimilation, Colonialism, and the Mexican American People*. Austin: Center for Mexican American Studies, 1975.

Murray, Thomas E. "Spanish Loanwords in Contemporary American English Slang." *Spanish Loanwords in the English Language: A Tendency Towards Hegemony Reversal*. Ed. Felix Rodriguez Gonzalez. Topics in English Linguistics 18. Berlin: Mouton, 105–37.

Nagy, William E., Erica F. McClure, and Montserrat Mir. "Linguistic Transfer and the Use of Context by Spanish-English Bilinguals." *Applied Psycholinguistics* 18.4 (1997): 431–52.

Norment, Nathaniel, Jr. "Quantitative Analysis of Cohesive Devices in Spanish and Spanish ESL in Narrative and Expository Written Texts." *Language Quarterly* 33.3–4 (1995): 135–59.

Olmos, Edward James, Lea Ybarra, Manuel Monterey, and Carlos Fuentes, eds. *Americanos: Latino Life in the United States*. Boston: Little Brown, 1999.

Pease-Alvarez, Lucinda, Kenji Hakuta, and Robert Bayley. "Spanish Proficiency and Language Use in a California Mexicano Community." *Southwest Journal of Linguistics* 15.1–2 (1996): 137–51.

Peña, Sylvia C. "Spanish as a Medium of Instruction in Bilingual Programs." *Language and Language Use: Studies in Spanish*. Ed. Terrell A. Morgan, James F. Lee, and Bill Van Patten. Lanham, MD: UP of America, 1987. 195–207.

Portales, Marco. *Crowding Out Latinos: Mexican Americans in Public Consciousness*. Philadelphia: Temple UP, 2000.

Rodriguez, Richard. "Bilingual Education: Outdated and Unrealistic." *Language: Readings in Language and Culture*. Ed. Virginia P. Clark, Paul A. Eschholz, and Alfred F. Rosa. New York: St. Martin's, 1998. 479–82.

———. *Hunger of Memory: The Education of Richard Rodriguez*. New York: Bantam, 1982.

Suro, Robert. *Strangers among Us: Latinos' Lives in a Changing America*. New York: Random/Vintage, 1999.

Valdés, Guadalupe. "Bilinguals and Bilingualism: Language Policy in an Anti-Immigrant Age." *International Journal of the Sociology of Language* 127 (1997): 25–52.

Winsler, Adam, Rafael M. Diaz, Linda Espinosa, and James L. Rodriguez. "When

Learning a Second Language Does Not Mean Losing the First: Bilingual Language Development in Low-Income, Spanish-Speaking Children Attending Bilingual Preschool." *Child Development* 70 (1999): 349–62.

Zentella, Ana Celia. "The Language Situation of Puerto Ricans." *Language Diversity: Problem or Resource?* Ed. Sandra Lee McKay and Sau-ling Cynthia Wong. Cambridge, MA: Newbury, 1988. 140–65.

Contributors

ARNETHA F. BALL is an associate professor of education at Stanford University. Her background includes work as a classroom teacher, speech pathologist, consultant, educational administrator, and teacher educator. Her research interests focus on how oral language and written literacies relate to culturally and linguistically diverse populations and also on the preparation of teachers to work with students who are poor, members of racially or ethnically marginalized groups, and speakers of first languages other than mainstream or academic English. Widely published, she explores the ways in which teachers use the language that students bring into the classroom as a resource. She is attempting to identify untapped literacy-related resources within the school and community context for use in the design of alternative instruction for diverse students.

SURESH CANAGARAJAH is an associate professor in the English department of Baruch College (City University of New York) where he teaches postcolonial writing, ESL, and composition. He previously taught for several years in Sri Lanka. His research relating to African American students appears in *College Composition and Communication*. His book *Resisting Linguistic Imperialism in English Teaching* won the Mina P. Shaughnessy Award (2000) of the Modern Language Association. In two of his books, *A Geopolitics of Academic Writing* and *Critical Academic Writing and Multilingual Students*, Canagarajah critiques the dominant practices in academic literacy.

VICTORIA CLIETT is completing a doctorate in English with an emphasis in rhetoric and composition studies. She is the 1996 recipient of the Conference on College Composition and Communication's Scholars for the Dream Travel Award. She is currently a learning specialist at Wayne State University.

KIM BRIAN LOVEJOY is an associate professor of English at Indiana University–Purdue University Indianapolis, where he teaches writing courses at the undergraduate and graduate levels. He has recently begun to offer an upper-division course, Issues in Teaching Writing, for practicing teachers of writing. He is the associate and managing editor of the *Journal of Teaching Writing* and coauthor of *Writing: Process, Product, and Power,* as well as the author of articles on academic writing, language diversity, revision, and portfolios.

RASHIDAH JAAMİ̀ MUHAMMAD is a professor of English and secondary education and is the academic coordinator of English programs at Governors State University, where she teaches graduate and undergraduate courses in American, African American, and young adult literatures, African American English, and English teaching methods. She is the coeditor (with Diane DuBose Brunner) of the SUNY Series *Urban Voices, Urban Visions.* Brunner and Muhammad recently completed *Zones of Contest,* a book on narrative practices in education.

GAIL Y. OKAWA is an associate professor of English at Youngstown State University. She was recently a scholar-in-residence at the Smithsonian Institution and is a former visiting scholar at the Center for Biographical Research, University of Hawaiʻi–Manoa. She is interested in the relationships among language/literacy, culture, and race in educational, historical, and political contexts. She has examined how these relationships can be manifested especially in teaching and learning and in teaching workforce issues in recent collections like *Race, Rhetoric, and Composition* and *Language Ideologies*, volume 1, as well as in "Diving for Pearls: Mentoring as Cultural and Activist Practice among Academics of Color" in *College Composition and Communication* 53 (2002): 507–30. Her current projects include a study of U.S. language history through objects in the Smithsonian collections and a study of the politics of language and identity among Japanese American immigrants who were incarcerated in U.S. Department of Justice internment camps during World War II.

DAVE PRUETT is a doctoral student at Texas A&M University, where he is completing a dissertation on Native American oral and written discourses in English: "Writing the Life of the Self: Constructions of Identity in Autobiographical Discourse by Six Eighteenth-Century American Indians." He is the associate editor of *Rhetoric, the Polis, and the Global Village.*

ELAINE RICHARDSON is an assistant professor of English and Applied Linguistics at Pennsylvania State University. Her ongoing research focuses on African American Language, literacy and culture, composition and rhetoric, hip hop, and discourse studies. Currently, her major interest is in literacy studies, more specifically in how African American English–speaking students' home language and culture can be used in literacy education. Another area of interest is computer technology and how it is used by people of Color in their work, lives, and communities. She is the author of the monograph *African American Literacies* and the coedited collections *Understanding African American Rhetoric* and *African American Rhetoric(s): Interdisciplinary Perspectives.* She has published various articles in books and in journals such as *College Composition and Communication* and the *Journal of Pidgin and Creole Languages.*

GENEVA SMITHERMAN (aka "Dr. G.") is University Distinguished Professor of English, the director of the African American Language and Literacy Program, and the director of "My Brother's Keeper" Program at Michigan State University. Internationally known for her work on African American Language and the *King* ("Black English") federal court case, she is author or editor/coeditor of thirteen books and over one hundred articles on language and education, including the classic work *Talkin and Testifyin: The Language of Black America.* She has been active in the Conference on College Composition and Communication and the National Council of Teachers of English for over twenty-five years and currently chairs the Language Policy Committee of CCCC. Noted for her educational activism, she received CCCC's Exemplar Award in 1999 and the David H. Russell Research Award from NCTE in 2001.

C. JAN SWEARINGEN is a professor of English at Texas A&M University and served as the president of the Rhetoric Society of America from 1998 to 2000. She recently coedited *Rhetoric, the Polis, and the Global Village,* a collection of essays from the RSA conference of 1998. Her book *Rhetoric and Irony, Western Literacy and Western Lies,* shared the W. Ross Winterowd Award for the outstanding book in composition theory published in 1991 from the *Journal of Advanced Composition.* Her research and teaching focus on the history and theory of rhetoric and composition, cross-cultural and comparative literary studies, and the influence of oral traditions and speech genres on written discourse in the classroom and in various literatures.

VICTOR VILLANUEVA is a professor and the chair of the Department of English at Washington State University, where he also teaches rhetoric and composition studies. He is the editor of *Cross-Talk in Comp Theory: A Reader,* now in its second edition, and the winner of two national awards on research and scholarship for his *Bootstraps: From an American Academic of Color.* He has written nearly forty articles, many of which have been anthologized. A popular speaker, he has delivered nearly sixty oral presentations, more than thirty-five of which have been keynotes, leading to his having been named Rhetorician of the Year in 1999. He is the former chair of the Conference on College Composition and Communication and has twice cochaired the organization's Winter Workshop. His concern is always with racism and with the political more generally—all as embodied in rhetoric and literacy.

Index

Studies in Writing & Rhetoric

In 1980 the Conference on College Composition and Communication established the Studies in Writing & Rhetoric (SWR) series as a forum for monograph-length arguments or presentations that engage general compositionists. SWR encourages extended essays or research reports addressing any issue in composition and rhetoric from any theoretical or research perspective as long as the general significance to the field is clear. Previous SWR publications serve as models for prospective authors; in addition, contributors may propose alternate formats and agendas that inform or extend the field's current debates.

SWR is particularly interested in projects that connect the specific research site or theoretical framework to contemporary classroom and institutional contexts of direct concern to compositionists across the nation. Such connections may come from several approaches, including cultural, theoretical, field-based, gendered, historical, and interdisciplinary. SWR especially encourages monographs by scholars early in their careers, by established scholars who wish to share an insight or exhortation with the field, and by scholars of color.

The SWR series editor and editorial board members are committed to working closely with prospective authors and offering significant developmental advice for encouraged manuscripts and prospectuses. Editorships rotate every five years. Prospective authors intending to submit a prospectus during the 2002 to 2007 editorial appointment should obtain submission guidelines from Robert Brooke, SWR editor, University of Nebraska-Lincoln, Department of English, P.O. Box 880337, 202 Andrews Hall, Lincoln, NE 68588-0337.

General inquiries may also be addressed to Sponsoring Editor, Studies in Writing & Rhetoric, Southern Illinois University Press, P.O. Box 3697, Carbondale, IL 62902-3697.